Praise for Clyde Fessler and *Rebuilding the Brand*

I have had the opportunity to observe a number of "marketing/brand management experts" across diverse industries over the last forty years but have never seen the likes of Clyde Fessler's creativity in defining and bringing to life the concept of "radical marketing and branding" strategies. People in the motorcycle industry laughed at his approach to marketing challenges, but they ridicule no more. His outside-the-box solutions boosted consumer confidence, and significantly improved market share brought about the creation of new products. His creativity and tenacity, combined with the talent of Rich Teerlink and other colleagues at Harley-Davidson, laid the foundation for significant increases in shareholder value. If you want your organization to preempt the competition, read this book.

—Bill Gray, retired VP of Human Resources, Harley-Davidson Motor Company

Clyde was truly one of the greatest leaders in Harley-Davidson's history. He helped lead Harley-Davidson to its current position as one of the top 100 brands in the world with market share leadership in virtually every customer segment. He always challenges conventional thinking and was a pioneer of the "close to the customer" philosophy of marketing. He lives with the customer and understands the customer better than anyone. There is a lot of wisdom in this book. It should be required reading for any business school marketing class.

—Jeff Merten, Former Vice President and General Manager, North American Sales, Harley-Davidson Motor Company

This incredible book gives you a good idea of how effective Clyde Fessler has been in helping to make Harley the amazing success story it has become. He gets what we motorcyclists are all about. His idea of a vacation is riding his bike to Sturgis, or Laconia, or maybe Daytona. He understands the customer and knows how much we love Harley bikes, because he shares that love with us. Thanks for all you've given us, Clyde. May the adventure continue and the good times keep rollin'!

—Pat Simmons, Doobie Brothers

Harley-Davidson may not have experienced 100 plus years of uninterrupted production without Clyde Fessler. I understand that this is a bold statement and that there were many thousands of individuals, from company men and women to dealers to the vital brand-loyal customers who held in there when the product was substandard and the company unresponsive to their needs. Clyde's legacy with Harley-Davidson is that he created the innovative programs and products that spread this intensely vertical brand and created products and services that anyone could embrace.

Rebuilding the Brand is a testament to Clyde, the focused, educated, endeavored individualist who burst through walls of dogma to see that "turning left" will set you free. It is also about building a brand, now one of the world's most recognized and popular brands, that at one time was primarily known as the motorcycle of choice for ruffians. Grandmothers didn't buy motorcycle T-shirts for their precious grandchildren before Clyde Fessler. They do now.

Lastly, this book is a great read from a colorful, engaging, deliciously intellectual man who has lived his life, twisted the throttle and flat out spread the love about a product the world now embraces.

—Dean V. Bordigioni, Bordigioni Family Winery, LLC

Clyde and I rode together for the first time in the early 1980s when Jefferson Starship had a gig at Summerfest in Milwaukee, Wisconsin, and we have been riding together ever since. When the band went their separate ways, it was Clyde's marketing strategy at Harley-Davidson of "turning left when the competition turns right" that led me to a second career. His advice really helped me stand out and be noticed above the crowd. Not only for the unique brand-building ideas, but for Clyde's many pearls of wisdom, *Rebuilding the Brand* is a must-read book.

—Craig Chaquico, former Jefferson Starship guitarist

Rebuilding the Brand is a textbook study of the Harley-Davidson turnaround, saving the brand, and making Harley-Davidson the King of the Road. The book would make a great textbook case study at every business school in the nation.

—Robert W. Miller, Executive Chairman, TH-INK TECH, INC.

It was the fall of 1986, I was the cofounder/editor of a brand-new motor-cycle magazine called *Harley Women*. My partner in the magazine and I had a meeting with the big boys at Harley-Davidson in Milwaukee. I was nervous . . . we were going to meet their Marketing Director, Clyde Fessler, for the first time. Cut to Sturgis, 1988. The magazine was going well, and our MotorClothes for women line was gaining speed. I ran into Clyde in the parking lot of the Super 8 motel in Sturgis. He was so passionate! I could tell he understood what women riders wanted and needed. Harley-Davidson was finally going to make clothing for us women! Clyde not only lives Harleys, but everything that goes with them. His enthusiasm is contagious and continues to encourage me today.

—Cris Sommer Simmons

REBUILDING THE
BRAND

HOW HARLEY-DAVIDSON
BECAME KING *of the* ROAD

CLYDE FESSLER

ALLWORTH PRESS
NEW YORK

Allworth Press books may be purchased in bulk at special discounts for
sales promotion, corporate gifts, fund-raising, or educational purposes.
Special editions can also be created to specifications. For details, contact
the Special Sales Department, Allworth Press, 307 West 36th Street, 11th
Floor, New York, NY 10018 or info@skyhorsepublishing.com.

17 16 15 14 13   5 4 3 2 1

Published by Allworth Press, an imprint of Skyhorse Publishing, Inc.
307 West 36th Street, 11th Floor, New York, NY 10018.

Allworth Press® is a registered trademark of Skyhorse Publishing, Inc.®,
a Delaware corporation.

www.allworth.com

Cover and interior design by Jenn Taylor

Library of Congress Cataloging-in-Publication Data is available on file.

Print ISBN: 978-1-62153-425-9
Ebook ISBN: 978-1-62153-422-8

Printed in the United States of America

This book is dedicated to the love of my life, my wife, Joan, my best friend and a true partner. Her inspiration, guidance, and support have led me to new horizons, a new career, and this book. They would not have happened without her.

One hundred percent of the royalties from the sale of this book will be divided between the Muscular Dystrophy Association and the Children's Hospital of South Dakota.

ACKNOWLEDGMENTS

Many thanks to all the great people at Harley-Davidson who supported me over the years, especially during the difficult times. Special thanks to Pat Thomson and Karen Poulos, executive assistants who made me look good and covered my . . . back.

Special appreciation and thanks to the marketing team of Kal Lawler, Mike Keefe, and Joanne Bischmann; each played an integral role in making it possible for Harley-Davidson to be inducted into the Marketing Hall of Fame.

Thanks to riding buddies:

Vaughn Beals

Jimmy Blazek

Dean Bordigioni

Craig Chaquico

Karen Fessler

Chuck Graves

Bill Gray

Jeff Merten

Rob Miller

Tom Parsons

Dick Pollick

Harlan Schillinger and all the Hamsters

Cris and Pat Simmons

Rich Teerlink

Thanks to racing buddies:

Scott Parker

Randy Goss

Jay Springsteen

Bill Werner

In memory of:

    Click Baldwin, Harley-Davidson dealer in Gastonia, North Carolina

    Dennis Maguire, founder of Boot Hill Saloon, Daytona Beach, Florida

    Gus Roenitz, lifelong friend, Sheboygan, Wisconsin

    Bruce Rossmeyer, Harley-Davidson dealer, Daytona, Florida, and multiple other locations

    Carlo Talamo, managing director of Numero Uno Harley-Davidson, Italy

Professional kudos to:

    Robert Grede, writer and author

    Robb Clouse, publisher

    Kirk Topel, owner of Hal's Harley-Davidson, Milwaukee, Wisconsin

TABLE OF CONTENTS

HARLEY-DAVIDSON CHRONOLOGY: 1978–1996

1978 ——————| "Turn left" strategy developed

1980 ——————| Tie in with Muscular Dystrophy Association charity

1981 ——————| Management buyout from American Machine and Foundry
Carmichael Lynch selected as lead advertising agency
Harley Owners Group established

1982 ——————| Harley reports loss of $20 million

1983 ——————| Bonus Bucks program launched
Harley has a 23 percent market share of heavyweight bikes
Harley reports loss of $30 million
Tariffs on Japanese bikes instituted

1984 ——————| Licensing strategy developed

1985 ——————| Harley-Davidson comes close to bankruptcy
Worldwide trademark registration plan created

1986 ——————| Harley refinances with Heller Financing
MotorClothes concept launched in Europe
Designer Store Program launched

1987 ——————| Harley requests lift of tariffs

1988 ——————| Harley has 47 percent market share of heavyweight bikes

1989 ——————| MotorClothes business group developed

1993 ——————| Ten-year strategic plan developed for Europe

1994 ——————| 2× in 3, 3× in 5 plan developed for Motor Accessories

1996 ——————| Rider's Edge program developed and launched

INTRODUCTION

I just happened to be in the right place at the right time.

Maybe I was the right guy for the circumstances, or maybe I just got lucky. It's probably some of both. When I joined Harley-Davidson as advertising and promotions manager in 1977, I was thirty-five years old. Little did I know what was in store for me and the company over the next twenty-five years.

I grew up in Sheboygan, Wisconsin, where my father had a small business—actually, several businesses. In one of his entrepreneurial adventures, he rented railroad passenger cars and organized day trips to Chicago Cubs baseball games. During the three-hour train ride to the Windy City, he held games of chance—a spinning wheel or some other carnival-type game—and earned enough to pay for the transportation and baseball tickets with something left over. I went along on some of those trips and collected the money and sold raffle tickets. It was a valuable learning experience in marketing, promotion, and salesmanship.

In high school, I was referred to as the Fonz. Leather jacket, long hair, black '51 customized Ford with dual exhausts and moon hubcaps. Mr. Cool. When I got caught smoking on school grounds, they suspended me from school athletics. So instead of playing varsity sports, I got involved in Catholic Youth Organization sports, student government, school plays, and planning events—homecoming, dances, the prom. When the high school sports teams played away games, I lined up buses to take students to the games. It was a good way to make a few bucks, and it taught me a lot about teamwork and how to motivate people.

At Notre Dame, I majored in English and finance and had my eye on law school, but I was still a bit of a rabble-rouser at heart; I even got arrested in Fort Lauderdale on spring break. After graduation, I purchased my first bike, a Honda 90—not what the Fonz would have ridden, but it got me around.

Law school bored me, or maybe I was just tired of going to school. After basic training in the National Guard, I got my first job with Kohler Company. We sold air-cooled engines to original equipment manufacturers in different industries—construction, power generation, landscaping, snowmobiles. Kohler taught me a lot about engines, transmissions, and recreational equipment.

After five years, I went to work for Arctic Cat, which makes snowmobiles in Thief River Falls, Minnesota. I traveled a lot, working with their dealership network. My job included the development of advertising campaigns, sales promotions, and dealer incentives. I also got to work with their racing team. Arctic Cat gave me a lifelong passion for recreational machines.

When it became evident that the snowmobile industry had peaked, I answered an ad for product manager at Harley-Davidson. They felt my background would be better suited for advertising and offered me the job of advertising and promotions manager, reporting to the director of marketing services. That was 1977, four years before thirteen of Harley-Davidson's top brass purchased the company from American Machine and Foundry (AMF) in a leveraged buyout.

By 1979, I was head of marketing services. In 1985, as Harley was on the verge of bankruptcy, our general sales manager left the company, and I was appointed the new general sales manager. I held several other positions over the years—such as director of licensing, VP of MotorClothes®, VP of general merchandise, VP of Motor Accessories, and managing director of Europe—until I became vice president of business development in 1996, the job I held until retirement in 2002.

So that's the résumé. Learning promotions at an early age, getting a financial education at college, understanding engines, and working with dealerships and their marketing requirements served as ideal preparation for what was to come. The rest, as they say, is history.

Many histories have been written about the Harley-Davidson company and its phoenix-like rise from the ashes of near bankruptcy to its laudable position among worldwide corporations today. There are histories of how Harley overcame the huge quality gap that existed between their bikes and Japanese bikes, histories of how Harley fought through crippling cash-flow problems and bankers ready to pull the plug, and histories of how Harley managed to out-Japanese the Japanese manufacturing methods of employee involvement, just-in-time inventory, and statistical operator control. But this is not another history book.

Rebuilding the Brand: How Harley-Davidson Became King of the Road is about branding. It is the story of how the marketing team at Harley took a brand whose image was downright awful and changed it, built it into the iconic brand the company enjoys today. I describe the methods we used to change the image, create more sales, build cash flow, and leave a legacy for generations of riders to come. At the core of our methods was the concept of "turning left" when the competition turned right. In effect, Harley-Davidson turned away from the path the competition took and went in a different direction.

This is not *my* story. It may be my perspective, the way I remember it, but it is truly the story of a group of talented and determined people—employees, dealers, and customers—who came together for a common purpose: to preserve the Harley-Davidson legacy so that the Bar and Shield, and all that it represents, might be held up as a model and admired the world over.

1
BRAND EXPERIENCE

Imagine: You rise up on your toes, bring your foot down hard on the starter of the classic XLCH Sportster, and hear the familiar "potato, potato, potato" of the engine. Your fingers grasp the handlebars, and a vibration runs the length of your arms and over your shoulders, until it melds with the rhythm of your heart. A twitch of your thumb and the engine roars. Your body shakes, and your knees flex to grasp the power between them. You settle into your seat and prepare for the journey.

In moments, the landscape glides past, and your senses are assaulted—the green of the grass and the bright blue sky, the tart smell of an orange grove or the musk of newly mown hay, the rising sun reflected in a clear mountain lake, or the serenity of a meadow of mustard grass gently waving in a soft breeze.

You are riding a Harley-Davidson motorcycle, and you are one with the bike.

It is an experience like no other, and it is crucial to the selling of Harley-Davidson motorcycles. To a true Hog, it is never about the destination. It is forever about the journey. It is the ride itself that matters. Once that is understood, the marketing of motorcycles becomes obvious.

What Is Brand Experience?

According to some heavily degreed academics named Brakus, Schmitt, and Zarantonello, "Brand experience is conceptualized as sensations, feelings, cognitions, and behavioral responses evoked by brand-related stimuli that are part of a brand's design and identity, packaging, communications, and environments."[1] In short, brand experience equals the sum of all points of contact with a brand. This includes both empirical evidence (how well the product performs) and peer assessments (how our friends and colleagues feel about the brand).

To produce a good experience, the brand must have personality.

A Very Brief History of Motorcycles

Most motorcycle makers grew out of the bicycle business—add an engine to a bicycle, and an industry is born. Harley-Davidson began in a Milwaukee garage in 1903.

The industry prospered and grew as more people sought inexpensive transportation—until the Great Depression. Suddenly, no one could afford to buy anything. Only two American motorcycle companies survived: Indian and Harley-Davidson. Shortly after World War II, Indian stopped making motorbikes.

During the 1950s and '60s, a few European bikes made their way to America, notably the English Triumph and the Italian Aermacchi, even a few German BMWs. But Harley had most of the market to itself.

Enter the Japanese. In the 1960s and '70s, Honda, Yamaha, Suzuki, and Kawasaki began selling motorcycles in the United States. Initially, they were not seen as a threat; they had no dealer network, and their bikes were small and technologically limited. But that quickly changed. Soon Japanese bikes flooded the market, and not just the small ones— big heavyweights, too. Honda alone built its brand to a 65 percent market share.

Until 1981. That's when Harley-Davidson started to fight back.

Brand Personality

We form opinions of other people based on their personalities and how we interact with them. Likewise, we form opinions of a brand based on its personality and how we interact with that brand—our brand experiences.

Every brand develops a personality over time. If people like the brand's personality, they buy it. If they like it a lot, they tell their friends and become loyal to that brand. They can't be lured away by price or promotion or anything else a competitor might throw at them. Ultimately, the better the personality and the more people who like that personality, the further the brand sets itself apart from competitors.

To create a personality that customers are going to like, you have to closely align your brand personality with your customers' personality. For instance, people not only buy motorcycles for transportation but also to fulfill their need for self-expression and individualism. So aligning Harley-Davidson with "rugged individualism" was critical to creating and maintaining the brand's personality.

Here are four steps to add personality to any brand:

1.   Make certain that the performance of the product or service is at least acceptable. Preferably, the product or service has a reputation for good quality. Without that, you're going to struggle.

2.   Create a story or stories attached to the brand. The more mythical and surreal the stories, the better.

3.   Turn left. Offer some sort of cultural contradiction, a mismatch between the accepted norm and what the brand has to offer.

4.   Make sure the brand maintains its personality. Engage your customers on an ongoing basis. Create new myths and stories. Brand personality is a living thing; it must be fed and nurtured.

The Harley Personality

In the first few decades following World War II, Harleys leaked oil and were frequently in the shop for repairs. Empirical evidence showed a slow, poor-quality product. The general public saw Harley riders as rowdy hooligans, grubby and unkempt. In short, the brand personality of a Harley-Davidson was dirty, sloppy, and nasty, a personality that was not likely to win many friends (customers).

How had this happened?

Veterans returning from World War II sought respite from the dull (comparatively) 1950s by riding their motorcycles throughout the countryside and raising hell in the process. They formed tribes—Pagans, Outlaws, Hells Angels—and lived a life of adventure on the road. Having no new motorcycles to ride (all had gone to the war effort), they bought prewar bikes and chopped them up to suit their taste, removing fenders to lighten the bikes, changing the bore and stroke dimensions to create more horsepower, adding free-flow exhausts and free-flow air cleaners and custom seats, and most impressive, extending handlebars to outrageous lengths. These modified bikes became known as "choppers."

Several motion pictures helped define the roughneck image of the motorcycle rider. In *The Wild One* (1953) starring Marlon Brando, biker Johnny Strabler and his motorcycle gang terrorize a sleepy California town. Loosely based on a true story of a band of hooligans terrorizing Hollister, California, *The Wild One* reflected society's growing fear of motorcycle gangs and motorcycle riders in general. (Ironically, though biker gangs are more often associated with Harleys, Brando rode a Triumph motorcycle in the movie.)

Other motorcycle movies further fed the anxiety. *The Wild Angels* (1966) and *Hells Angels on Wheels* (1967) starring Peter Fonda and Jack Nicholson, respectively, led to one of the most famous biker movies of all time, *Easy Rider* (1969), starring both Fonda and Nicholson. Harley-Davidson motorcycles figured prominently in each movie and helped foster an image of evil and discontent. Motorcycle riders, particularly those who rode Harleys, were unsavory lawbreakers.

Meanwhile, Japanese bikes, which began flooding the US market in the 1960s and '70s, developed their own personality—sleek and fast. They ran seemingly forever without breaking down or leaking oil, the perfect utilitarian vehicle for everyday transportation.

To top it off, in 1964, Honda Motorcycles launched their famous ad campaign: "You Meet the Nicest People on a Honda." The Honda 50 was portrayed as a casual vehicle for daily activities—Mom picking up groceries or Dad taking young Johnny to Little League. This was an entirely new way to view motorcycles, as an alternative mode of transportation sold as family value. It portrayed Honda—and Honda customers—in direct contrast to the rough, tough Harley image. The campaign was a success. During the 1970s, Honda grew rapidly and soon dominated the American motorcycle market.

At about that same time, *Cycle* magazine wrote a scathing review of Harley-Davidson motorcycles. The article concluded that Harley-Davidson made "prehistoric hogs." The image stuck.

Harleys thus became known as hogs—big, fat, slow, and sloppy. They leaked oil and often were ridden by dirty, malfeasant roughnecks. Quick, what's the difference between a Hoover vacuum cleaner and a Harley-Davidson motorcycle? The Harley holds two dirtbags.

The Route to Quality

In 1981, AMF sold the Harley-Davidson Motor Company to a group of thirteen investors led by Vaughn Beals and Willie G. Davidson (grandson of the founder) for $80 million. The buyout brought a sense of spirit to the company and breathed new life into the dealer network. For years, dealers had felt as if motorcycles were just another product in AMF's long line of sports and leisure goods, which included tennis rackets, bicycles, snowmobiles, exercise equipment, golf clubs, snow skis, sailboats, scuba gear, and more—all of which were promoted under a blanket slogan: "AMF. We make weekends."

This did not sit well with dealers. They didn't like that AMF made other products that competed with theirs. Dealers wanted AMF customers to spend their weekends on a Harley, not golfing or playing tennis. Their frustration boiled over when one of the animated AMF TV commercials showed a Harley motorcycle with the air intake and exhaust pipes on the wrong side. Dealers screamed for AMF to get it right or get out.

> "Harley-Davidson does not sell bikes. We sell the experience." So said Harley president Vaughn Beals in the early 1980s, when Harley faced its toughest years.[2]

The buyout also energized company employees. Attitudes and moods changed. The whole Milwaukee community embraced the independence of their hometown company. Newspaper headlines shouted, "The Eagle Soars Alone."

Harley management quickly recognized the problems they faced: poor economy, excess inventory, bad quality, poor image, no money. A lot needed to be fixed, but priorities had to be set. It didn't take long to see that the first priorities had to be *quality* and *cash flow*. Money talks, and often loudest. While financial considerations were paramount, quality had to be improved, or the company had no future. With quality improvement would come more sales, better cash flow, more profit, and financial security for the long term. So management tackled quality improvement first.

Quality stunk. The leaking oil and the frequent breakdowns were just what the customer saw. The problems went far deeper. Assembly lines in the Milwaukee and York, Pennsylvania, plants were cluttered with parts, tools, diagrams, and notes. Every few feet or so was another computer station for checking schedules and entering production figures.

Harley purchased parts in bulk to save money. "Economies of scale" they called it, but it didn't turn out that way. While the parts sat around waiting to be used on the assembly line, some of them got nicked or scratched. Some rusted. Others had been redesigned by the time they were ready to be used, so they didn't work properly or no longer fit.

Half the bikes coming off the assembly line had missing parts. Some sort of rework was required on nearly every bike. Unfinished bikes sat at the end of the line in an area that became known as "the hospital." Some sat there for weeks before they were repaired and ready to ship.

Meanwhile, the Japanese were building better bikes in a wider range of sizes, and they were doing it faster and cheaper than Harley-Davidson. How? How were they able to make more bikes, cheaper, and better? An American showed them how.

After World War II, when Japan was rebuilding its war-shattered economy, a relatively obscure quality expert named W. Edwards Deming introduced centralized decision making, just-in-time inventory management, and inspection-as-you-go quality control methods to Japanese business leaders. The techniques proposed by Deming offered distinct advantages to a country whose manufacturing plants had been completely destroyed. They could be learned easily; they cost little to introduce; and the manufacturing process required a minimum of cash.

American executives, on the other hand, viewed these techniques as manufacturing tricks and deemed them unnecessary. Managers assumed they would have to change existing processes that were already profitable. Besides, the postwar market for products was booming; returning veterans and their growing families bought more products each year. Offshore competition was negligible.

But by 1981, that had changed. Harley needed to learn and adapt these "Japanese" methods, and they had to do it quickly. Harley-Davidson management called up its chief competitor and arranged to take a tour of a Honda motorcycle manufacturing plant. (I will never understand why Honda honored our request. Today it would be called corporate intelligence gathering or even industrial spying—after all, we were blatantly going there to learn how their business operated—but at the time, it was simply positioned as a goodwill gesture.)

The trip to Marysville, Ohio, was an eye-opener. Compared to Harley's factory, the Honda assembly line was neat and uncluttered. The factory floor was not littered with vast supplies of parts waiting to be used in assembly. There were few inspectors weeding out defective products, few managers fixing scheduling problems, and little paperwork. And there were no computers. None. Harley, by comparison, had a complex computer program that required input at multiple stages along the line, which slowed down the work in process.

More than anything, the Honda plant tour pointed out the stark contrast between the quality of Japanese bikes and the quality of Harley-Davidson bikes. Only 5 percent of motorcycles coming off the Honda assembly line were defective, compared to over 50 percent at Harley.

> "We were being wiped out by the Japanese because they were better managers. It wasn't robotics, or culture, or morning calisthenics and company songs. It was professional managers who understood their business and paid attention to detail."[3]
>
> —Vaughn Beals

Bottom line: the basic production processes at Harley were flawed. So that's where management placed its emphasis. Quality had to improve. The Milwaukee and York plant managers met with workers' representatives over several months in 1981, not only to build consensus on what changes would need to be made, but also to ease skepticism. Union representatives were particularly suspicious, worried that changes might lead to layoffs or reduced wages.

While there were some starts and stops—not everyone bought into the process—ultimately quality began to improve through a combination of changes that came to be known as the productivity triad:

1. **Employee involvement (EI)**—Empower all employees at all levels of the company to identify and solve problems.

2. **Just-in-time inventory (JIT)**—Eliminate large parts inventories, and require vendor cooperation to deliver small quantities of parts as they are needed. Harley-Davidson called it "materials as needed" (MAN).

3. **Statistical operator control (SOC)**—Require employees to measure the quality of their production and keep track of any variances; "within tolerances" is not acceptable.

These three production methods were integral to the advances in quality at Harley-Davidson in the early 1980s. Harley enlisted the full participation of all employees in solving problems and controlling quality. Employees found themselves in an atmosphere of continuous improvement, one in which they were never satisfied with results that were less than perfect. Management pushed decision-making responsibility down the chain as far as possible and gave all employees the tools for monitoring and controlling the quality of their work.

Each employee had accountability for identifying problems and seeking solutions, rather than passing them down the line. SOC helped reduce scrap and defects by allowing employees to rework machines right on the assembly line. Workers established parameters for quality using statistical methods, and they charted their defect rates and introduced improvements with no management approval required.

Even though Harley lost $20 million that first year in business, the company had a positive cash flow of $5 million. How? We managed to take $25 million out of inventory with the new JIT policy. Vendor cooperation was critical; vendors had to deliver smaller quantities and spread deliveries over longer periods. The lack of disarray on the assembly line and the fewer parts waiting to be installed helped ensure a brisk work flow, and the resulting improvement in cash flow bought the company the time it needed to recover.

These three basic ideas—EI, JIT, and SOC—transformed Harley-Davidson motorcycles from mechanical nightmares to reliable bikes. While the quality problems did not disappear overnight, they were clearly on the mend. The results were nothing short of amazing. Productivity improved over 50 percent. Scrap and rework were reduced by two-thirds. JIT reduced inventories 75 percent, which, as mentioned, had a huge impact on cash flow.

As a company, Harley-Davidson believed first and foremost in being honest with its customers. A big part of that honesty was to admit our mistakes. If you screw up—and we did—face up to it. Show your customers how you are fixing the problems. Then move on.

So that's what we did. First, we fixed the quality problems. Then we apologized to all our dealers; they were the ones saddled with repairing all those poorly made bikes before delivery to the customers. We followed that with big, colorful magazine ads that apologized to our customers. We turned negatives into positives.

And then we moved on.

Bonding with Customers

As advertising and promotions manager, it was my job to know our customers. I looked around and saw the ugly brand personality of Harley. Poor quality. Unsavory riders. Hogs. It was all true. The experiences our customers were having with the brand stunk, too.

I came face to face with these unruly customers at my first bike rally in Daytona, Florida. It was the late 1970s, and the police were having trouble keeping the hell-raising bikers separated from the college kids on spring break who wanted to raise some hell of their own.

I had only been with Harley-Davidson a few months, and Daytona was my trial by fire. The weeklong rally brought bikers from all over the world, at that time, about 45,000 riders; now, it's a quarter million or more. They all gathered on Main Street on the final Saturday night. That's when all the bikers showed off their iron—hundreds of Harleys handlebar to handlebar, chrome glittering like fireflies in the streetlights, all the mamas and all the dudes wearing leather. It was Mardi Gras on wheels. I had no clue.

But I sure was going to look good. In my hotel room, I slid into a pair of black dress slacks and put on my best John Travolta polyester shirt with my Harley factory pin in the collar. I was styling.

It wasn't long before one particular Harley caught my eye. Nearly twenty years old, it had been meticulously restored—rechromed, new paint, reconditioned leather seat. It looked awesome. So did the girl standing next to it. "Is this your bike?" seemed like an innocent question.

Then I noticed that the helmet she carried was about four sizes too big. Too late. From out of the dark came, "Hey, dude. Lay off my chick."

He was a monster—at least six feet plenty and 300 pounds of bone and sinew and anger. Clenched in his paw, a 16-ounce beer barely peeked between his massive fingers.

"I work for the factory," I said. "See my pin?"

He responded, "Know what I think of that?"

He picked me off my feet, buried his face in my shoulder, and spit out my Harley collar pin with a gravel-voiced "What do you think of that, dude?"

I tried not to. Before he could make a fist, I grabbed his hand and shook it. "Thank you for riding a Harley-Davidson motorcycle," I said.

I scurried back to my hotel room, where it didn't take long to dump the disco look and put on a black T-shirt with a pair of jeans. If you want to talk to bikers, you'd better look like a biker. Moreover, you had better *be* a biker. For the next five years, I stopped shaving at Thanksgiving. Before attending the Daytona rally each March, I made sure I looked the part of a biker. And I didn't fly to Florida; I rode. I took my staff so they could get out of the office and really get a feel for the brand experience our customers were having. Problems are in the office; solutions are in the field.

It was a valuable lesson. From that point on, this fundamental principle permeated everything we did as a company. It is not enough to get close to your customers; you have to bond with them. That bond begins with trust. You couldn't just dress like a biker, wear long hair, jeans, and a black T-shirt. You had to ride and be a biker. You can't talk bikes unless you understand the biker's life.

Harley-Davidson, All-American

At the time of the buyout in 1981, Harley-Davidson was the last remaining motorcycle manufacturer in America. If Harley died, there would be no more bikes made in the United States. With Japanese manufacturers dumping their surplus inventory on the US market, Harley was losing money—fast. It was questionable whether the company could continue.

But in 1982, Harley won a judgment from the International Trade Commission (ITC) that allowed the US government, under the urging of President Ronald Reagan, to increase tariffs on Japanese motorcycles, especially heavyweight bikes. The additional tariffs—45 percent on top of an existing 4.4 percent—gave Harley-Davidson the opportunity to revitalize, to make the changes needed to compete.

The Japanese manufacturers avoided some of the tariffs by building more machines in the United States and manufacturing motorcycles that had an engine size that was one cubic centimeter smaller than the tariff specifications. Some even went so far as to copy Harley's classic styling. They seemed to be trying to be more American, and while they may have been made in the United States, and even used classic American bike styling, they were still Japanese bikes.

Harley recognized the opportunity to capitalize on the copycat designs of the Japanese manufacturers. The company seized the chance to tout its heritage: rugged, adventurous, classic, and 100 percent American. Patriotism became our promotional strategy, a brand experience in a sense. All Harley-Davidson's advertising in those first few years used a "Made in America" theme.

We even went so far as to taunt the Japanese manufacturers. We ran colorful full-page ads in *Cycle* magazine with much of the copy translated into Japanese, suggesting that since the Japanese had been copying Harley's classic designs anyway, we might as well make sure that nothing got lost in the translation.

We gave all our dealers big welcome mats printed in Japanese. These served a dual purpose. First, they reinforced Harley-Davidson's heritage—made in America—with a gentle poke at the competition. Second, many dealers preferred not to sell to riders of Japanese bikes—didn't even want their bikes in their parking lots. Harley wanted to make it clear to the dealers that all motorcyclists are part of a riding brotherhood. We needed to convince dealers that if a biker rode into his lot, no matter what brand he rode that day, he was a bike rider and therefore might be converted to the Harley brand some day.

This ad campaign and accompanying promotional tools, along with our dealers' commitment, expanded our target market to include all bike riders. No longer were we just the bad boys of the biker world. We were going after those nice people you meet on a Honda, too.

HOG

People were buying Japanese bikes for transportation. They were cheap on gas and easier to park than a car. A Japanese bike would reliably get you from point A to point B.

Harley-Davidson management recognized that riding a Harley was an experience. At Harley-Davidson, we fulfilled dreams.

A comparison might look like this:

Why Buy a Japanese Bike?	Why Buy a Harley-Davidson Bike?
Utilitarian	Status
Logical	Emotional
Reliable transport	The journey

And so, while the Japanese were turning right, making utilitarian machines, we decided to turn left. We decided to sell brand experience.

If it's true that "you meet the nicest people on a Honda," then certainly it could be said that you meet bikers on a Harley. So why not use that?

The Daytona, Florida, rally was the catalyst. By the spring of 1982, the Daytona Police Department was ready to ban all bikers from Daytona Beach during the heavy spring break tourist season. If ever there was an oil-and-water combination, it was hard-core bikers and rich college kids.

The rally was important to Harley-Davidson. Its history dated to the 1930s; Daytona had served as a traditional gathering place for bikers from around the world. It was the perfect opportunity to meet riders, learn what they wanted in new bikes, and demonstrate all the new motorcycles and motorcycle accessories.

That was motivation enough, but Harley also saw an opportunity to become a leader in the minds of their target market. Harley management decided to meet with Daytona's chamber of commerce, the police, and Jim France of the Daytona Speedway to try to solve the problem. We agreed to work closely with them to provide something for the bikers to do (something other than drink beer and raise hell).

We offered to sponsor biker movies at the local theaters; we agreed to provide demonstration rides on new Harley-Davidson motorcycles; we arranged for accessories manufacturers to pay the chamber for the rights to erect tents to display their wares; and we organized a big parade to the Daytona Speedway for the race. It was a chance for all the bikers to ride down Main Street and show off their customized iron to one another.

Ultimately, it was a big hit. Fewer fights broke out (the police appreciated that), and the City of Daytona Beach still got all the revenue from both the kids and the bikers (the local businesses appreciated that). Accessories manufacturers got to show off their stuff. Harley-Davidson enjoyed a newfound status among the rider elite. Bikers got access to all the new bikes and accessories. Everybody was happy, a win-win.

This led to the development of a special club just for Harley-Davidson motorcycle owners. We figured bikers would want to hang out with fellow bikers. After all, many had been joining biker clubs or gangs for years. But we wanted to make a club for regular riders, not roughnecks looking for trouble. The club experience had to be fun and adventurous, sure, but it also had to be safe and family-friendly—like a country club on wheels. So we modeled it after the Greek system of fraternities and sororities and, to some degree, the American Automobile Association (AAA).

At a brainstorming session, we came up with a list of membership benefits:

- Have fun
- Be safe
- Belong to a community or tribe of like-minded people
- Have a reason to ride
- Get emergency road service (like AAA)
- Stay connected through a club newsletter

Wow, this sounded like a club we all wanted to belong to! Exciting, adventurous rides to interesting places with a group of like-minded riders to share the journey—fun! All we needed was a name. A good name, something catchy. We decided to turn a negative into a positive, and we called it the Harley Owners Group®, HOG for short.

HOG

A brainstorming session yielded the acronym.

The H was easy. That stood for Harley.

O = Outrageous? Organization? Optimist? Outgoing? Owner? *Owner* worked.

G = Go? Going? Gone? Gathering? Group?

Yes! Harley. Owners. Group. That was it!

And HOG was born.

Every purchase of a Harley-Davidson motorcycle enrolled the rider in Harley Owners Group for one year. (After the first year, riders paid a modest fee for annual membership.) This primed the pump, got riders involved, got dealers excited, and provided Harley-Davidson (and their local dealers) with a roster of riders to whom Harley could send rally invitations and other mailings.

Furthermore, Harley required every one of its dealers to sponsor at least one event, giving HOG members a multitude of destination choices and rider experiences. Harley fulfills dreams; you choose your dream.

Next, we created a unique patch or pin for each event. Like a Boy Scout merit badge, it gave riders a way to acknowledge their experiences and demonstrate their longevity and status. They also served as conversation pieces: "Oh, you were at Sturgis last year? How was it?"

Early on, we decided rallies should be built around the journey, not the destination: Coast to Coast, Canada to Mexico, Ride the Rockies. Take a trip through Monument Valley with a geologist who explains the various rock formations. Or follow Route 66, and meet with historians at various towns along the famous highway. Afterward, riders would talk about their experiences, their journeys. Over time, the club would create lasting connections among Harley owners. They would become friends with one another and look forward to future rides together—on their Harleys, of course.

"Everything is checked at the beginning of the ride—politics, beliefs, professions, education—none of that matters," says Kirk Topel, Harley-Davidson dealer in New Berlin, Wisconsin. "All that matters is the experience. Only members of religious organizations have a deeper bond for each other."

This bond is shared by Harley riders across the globe and creates a link between Harley customers and the Harley brand that is immutable, enduring, eternal—producing a positive brand experience.

Research shows that HOG members typically spend 30 percent more than other Harley riders on accessories, clothes, and Harley-Davidson-sponsored events.[4] HOG members are brand loyal. The nirvana for any good marketer: brand loyalty.

Begun in 1983, within four years there were over 100,000 HOG members. Eight years later, in 1991, HOG held its first official HOG rally in Europe, in Cheltenham, England. In 2008, HOG marked its 25th year during Harley-Davidson's 105th anniversary celebration in Milwaukee, Wisconsin. Today there are more than 1,400 chapters worldwide with over one million members.

Harley turned a negative into a positive by facing the ugly image of "hog" head-on and gave owners a reason to ride by creating HOG—a big part of the brand experience.

Rider's Edge

The brand connection truly begins when the rider buys a bike. But before he (or increasingly, she) can buy a bike, the prospective customer needs to know how to ride. We figured that if Harley were the ones who taught people how to ride, they would be more likely to buy a Harley.

Back in 1996, as now, the Motorcycle Safety Foundation® (MSF) sanctioned all rider training and licensing. To get your motorcycle license, you had to learn from an MSF-certified instructor through a state-sponsored program. Back then, many states had motorcycle instruction waiting lists. In Wisconsin, the wait was six to nine months; in Pennsylvania, you had one day to sign up or you'd wait a whole year; and in California, off-duty California Highway Patrol (CHP) officers taught the course, so they lobbied against any non-CHP certifications.

But we were determined to break down the barriers to certification and increase the number of motorcycle riders—and create more brand users in the process. So we identified our top ten dealers and asked them to roll out our motorcycle instruction program. We called it Rider's Edge®. Every one of our dealers was skeptical. Some wanted loans to finance the program. A few flat out refused to do it at all.

Could you blame them? It was a completely new business for dealers. They were being asked to hire MSF-certified instructors, find classroom facilities (their showrooms were not equipped to handle classroom seating), and devote a fleet of bikes specifically to training. They needed special liability insurance for the students, and they needed to find an empty parking lot in which to practice—a local church or school willing to tolerate the noise.

Sound like a recipe for disaster?

When students begin the Rider's Edge program, they are first given a dealer orientation. They meet the salespeople and the service mechanics. They're shown all the riding gear and given all the financing alternatives and insurance options. They are introduced to all the different Harley-Davidson motorcycles in the showroom.

Next, they spend twenty-five hours in a classroom learning road rules and safety skills. There are notes to take and laws to memorize, study guides, and tests.

Then, finally, the students get to ride the bikes. Frankly, the first ten minutes are often hilarious. But most soon get the hang of it, braking and turning, working the clutch, dodging orange cones, and righting a bike when it falls over. By the end of their hands-on tutelage, they may not be experienced riders, but they are competent, and they know how to handle a big bike. Most importantly, they are confident. They have lost that apprehension most new riders feel when they first get on a heavyweight motorcycle.

It didn't take long before the dealers embraced Rider's Edge. First, it served as a way to introduce new riders to the brand. Second, it created a comfort level for non-riders, those unfamiliar with bikes, or those unfamiliar with heavyweights. Third, it was an outstanding selling opportunity—dealers sold parts and accessories, and especially clothes, to the students. (As an added bonus, the program also encouraged riding couples and two-bike households, with all the clothes and accessories for each.) And most importantly, it taught riders how to ride their motorcycles safely, as well as motorcycle etiquette and rules of the road.

Rider's Edge has been a huge success. Today, over half of all dealers offer a licensing program. Rider's Edge makes bikes accessible to the average Joe (or Joan); it relieves non-bikers of the anxiety of that first ride; it introduces new riders to the brand; and it launches riders' lifelong partnerships with their dealer and with Harley-Davidson.

For many, Rider's Edge is their first Harley-Davidson brand experience.

The Super Ride Program

After the buyout, quality improved, and by 1986, most of the oil leaks and breakdowns were no longer prevalent. But many customers were still convinced that if it looked like a Harley, it must leak like a Harley. It was the brand experience they had come to expect. Harley had to change that perception.

We used a classic marketing solution: if you have a product that is unknown or misunderstood, sample; let your customers try the product for free.

That's exactly what the Super Ride program did. It allowed potential customers to take demonstration rides on the new bikes. They had a chance to see for themselves that Harleys no longer leaked oil. They could get a feel for how the new bikes handled. They could see, hear, and touch the quality firsthand. They could sample the Harley brand experience—the *new* brand experience—completely risk free.

Now, nothing is truly free. The whole purpose of the program was to sell bikes. In addition to months of preparation, we spent $3 million in television commercials just to promote the event. Over three weekends, Harley gave 90,000 rides to 40,000 prospective customers at rallies and dealerships. Many of the test rides were given to owners of Japanese bikes. In that respect, the program was a huge success. Forty thousand people sampled the new quality Harley. Unfortunately, not enough of them purchased motorcycles to pay for the program.

There were several reasons:

- Some dealers were poorly organized, resulting in long lines of frustrated would-be riders.

- Some offered demo rides on Saturdays and Sundays, but then they closed their stores by 2 p.m. and went riding.

- Other dealers just didn't know how to close a sale.

Despite our best efforts at headquarters on Juneau Avenue to distribute detailed instructions to the dealers on laying out their stores for the event, organizing the demo rides, and managing the crowds, we did not adequately train the dealers. All communication was one way; we didn't seek feedback, answer questions or concerns, or allow for consensus decisions.

Though that first program was a failure, it also had its benefits. It showed us that we needed to get closer to our dealer network and really teach them better sales techniques, show them how to be better businessmen. Most of our dealers, after all, were mechanics and riding enthusiasts. The first Super Ride program taught us that we had a long way to go in developing dealers' sales skills and business acumen (more on that in chapter 4). It also taught us that a demo program was necessary to sell more motorcycles.

The program's greatest impact was that it demonstrated to potential buyers that Harley's quality had returned. Though they did not buy bikes during that three-week period, many of those who took a demo ride later chose Harley-Davidson when they were ready for their next bike. Super Ride helped change the perceptions of a core group of customers. They now had a positive brand experience—and they would tell others.

2
BRAND EXTENSION

Imagine: The storm has passed. The smell of rain evaporating off the asphalt fills your senses as you accelerate into the late afternoon. A red sun still rests on the edge of the horizon. Great purple clouds roll east, in a hurry to catch up to the stabs of lightning still visible, but tiny, in your mirrors. Mist from the road spills across your windshield as your wheels pelt your back with road wash.

You smile. You're protected. You wear a Harley-Davidson jacket with the collar firmly tucked beneath your helmet. The water has nowhere to go but back to the ground from where it came.

And so the journey continues.

You purchased the leather jacket with the reflective piping and embroidered graphics just for times like these. It's waterproof. It's versatile. You like the snap-in vest you can wear under the jacket to keep you warm and the front and back vents that keep you cool.

It looks good, and you look good in it. But mostly, you bought it because it carries a brand name you trust.

What Is Brand Extension?

Brand extension—also called brand stretching or brand spin-off—uses a trusted brand name to sell more to a current base of customers. Brand extension significantly reduces the risks that come with introducing a new product line. It can also lure new customers to the brand with new products that would not ordinarily be associated with that brand. It is the single most effective marketing strategy for building sales at the least expense.

The Five Strategies

There are five and only five ways to grow a business:[5]

1. Buy market share.
2. Hunt new business.
3. Harvest your existing customer base.
4. Develop new products.
5. Merge with or acquire another company.

Brand extension harvests more sales from existing customers and lures (hunts) new customers.

A familiar brand comes with ready-made awareness and perceptions. It's much easier to leverage the success and popularity of a known brand when launching a new product, especially if it is to the same target market. Consumers are more likely to trust a new product (or a line of products) that has a brand name they trust.

For instance, Procter & Gamble's Ivory® soap has been around since 1879. The bar that floats (it's "99 and 44/100 percent pure") has launched myriad brand extensions, including liquid hand soap, shampoo, body wash, dishwashing liquid, hand lotion, and a mild laundry product called Ivory Snow.

Ivory soap has come to be associated with purity and gentleness. That is its brand personality. Procter & Gamble recognized the opportunity to extend that personality to other products—dishwashing liquid that was gentle on hands, shampoo that was gentle enough for children—without the heavy advertising and promotion expense required to create whole new personalities for those same products.

A promotional claim like "Pishposh Dishwashing Liquid is gentle on your hands" would be received with skepticism. No one knows anything about the Pishposh brand. Not so with "Ivory Dishwashing Liquid is gentle on your hands." Ivory is a trusted brand, and its brand personality is all about purity and gentleness.

Brand Extension at Nike

What do you know about Nike? They make shoes, right? At one time they made just athletic shoes, but now they make all kinds of shoes. Clothing, too.

How would you feel about a Nike energy drink? Or Nike cologne or body wash? What about a Nike workout center? You can bet they're all under consideration. Why? Because Nike is a trusted brand.

Nike became known the world over for making quality sports shoes. By extending its brand to include a variety of sport categories that all carry the Nike name, Nike is able to build upon its brand equity to increase sales.

There are many good reasons to extend your brand:

- Brand extensions reduce the costs and risks associated with introducing a new product. Your brand is already known and trusted. Use that. Present your new product to the same group of customers. Your customers will assume that your new product has the same level of quality as the parent brand. Customers will assign that credibility almost unconsciously.

- You save on promotion expense. Your target market is already aware of your brand name, so advertising heavily to create brand recognition and credibility is not necessary. Also, if you do advertise the new branded product, it adds to the interest in the parent brand and grows your customer base.

- Retailers give you a break. They are more likely to stock a new product with a known brand name on it. It's less risky for them. You get more shelf space than unknown brands.

- Brand extensions reduce a company's dependency on one product. If the parent brand's sales decline, the brand extension can pick up the slack. An example in the extreme: while demand for OshKosh B'gosh® bib overalls and farm outerwear began to decline in the 1980s, the company's brand extension into kid's clothing grew, and today, OshKosh B'gosh only makes clothes for kids.

It took time and money for Harley-Davidson to build brand trust. It took years to convert skeptical consumers, riders accustomed to oil leaks and poor performance, some afraid of the riders themselves. Extensive advertising and promotion campaigns positioned the brand as all-American, classic, adventuresome, and fun. The time and money were well spent; brand extension became integral to Harley's growth.

Your Customers First

In the early 1980s, our research showed that among those riders who owned a Harley, a majority would only consider buying another Harley and never look at any other brand of motorcycle. Even when they leaked or broke down, our customers remained true to Harley. They were loyal customers. They are loyal customers still. And they are our best salespeople.

Still today, a vast majority (back in the 1980s, it was over 75 percent) of Harley-Davidson advertising, public relations, and promotion dollars are aimed squarely at current Harley customers. Not the Japanese riders. Not non-riders. Harley riders.

It is easier to harvest sales from your current field of customers than it is to hunt new ones. Selling to your customers provides you with a distinct competitive advantage, making it easier to sell more of your products and services—your brand extensions.

There are many ways to sell more to your existing customers. Some common terms used in the business world include:

- Suggestive selling
- Rotation farming
- Incentive selling
- Selling complete systems
- Selling accessories

In a fast-food restaurant, you order a sandwich, and the cashier asks if you want fries with your order. That's called *suggestive selling*. Its purpose is to trigger an additional purchase. It's the easiest way for any brand to build sales. The customer is already in a buying mood. His wallet is open. You simply suggest he spend a little more money to enhance the quality of his original purchase. When a Harley dealer sells a bike, the salesperson will often suggest the handlebar grips, foot pegs, or custom seat. If the rider uses Harley-Davidson financing, the salesperson can wrap the accessories right into the total purchase price (that way, the customer finances the accessories, too, rather than paying cash for them separately).

Rotation farming is used for the customer who comes back on a regular basis, like someone going for a haircut or to the dentist. Many Harley dealers reach out to customers and schedule routine maintenance appointments—oil changes, brake adjustments, safety checks—each spring before riding season begins. Riders appreciate the reminder, and dealers earn extra revenue while further cementing relationships with their best customers, current Harley owners.

Incentive selling works on many levels. Free gifts, premiums, and discounts can all be used to build sales from your existing customer base. "Buy one, get one free!" always draws a crowd to fast-food restaurants and department store sales. Every time a rider buys a new Harley-Davidson motorcycle, he or she receives a free one-year membership in the Harley Owners Group. A dealer might even throw in a free jacket with the purchase of a new bike.

This is the age of convenience. People want easy turnkey operations. Savvy companies recognize that *selling complete systems* is a great way to grow more business. Harley dealers sell not just a piece of iron but a whole set of accompanying products and services, including beginner, skilled, and group riding instruction; motor accessories to customize your bike; motor clothing to suit your riding lifestyle; financing services; delivery arrangements; and maintenance and repair programs.

Selling accessories is especially effective when your brand has a loyal following. Many dealers mix and match products in their showrooms to show how different parts work together—the boots and hat that go with the jacket, the speaker lids that work best with the Boom!™ audio system, or the special Harley-Davidson motor oil that makes that V-twin hum. The customer is happy to receive this valuable advice; he learns what makes the item he just bought work better or look better. The dealers are happy because they have maximized their sales at better profit margins.

Marketing Strategy

At a brainstorming meeting not long after the buyout, we began developing a long-term plan that we believed would put Harley-Davidson on the track to success. We outlined Harley's core competencies and created a plan for increasing sales in other areas that we believed held the greatest opportunities.

We saw opportunities to build our business through non-motorcycle products. Clothing topped that list. We included Harley credit and Harley insurance and even had our eyes set on a Harley museum sometime down the road. Other future opportunities that we explored included cafés and diners, hotels, rider education, service centers, and collectibles, even theme parks.

Harley-Davidson Motor Accessories

The ability to extend a brand depends on how strongly your customers feel about the parent brand, the brand's quality, and its value.

In the early 1980s, people didn't feel real good about the Harley brand. The brand's image was as tarnished as an old V-twin carburetor. But slowly, ever so slowly, that changed. Quality began to improve dramatically. Harley reduced defects and scrap by reworking the bikes on the assembly line. The workers established quality parameters, kept track of their successes or failures, and introduced improvements right on the factory floor. No morning calisthenics or company songs, but very Japanese-like nonetheless.

Once the quality improved, it was really our customers who told us that we needed to extend the brand. They were already buying aftermarket accessories—such as luggage racks, customized seats, and windshields—from manufacturers who simply used Harley bike dimensions to build the add-ons and decorative trimmings. Whole industries dealing in Harley accessories had sprung up. Everybody was making money from selling Harley-Davidson motorcycle accessories—everybody except Harley-Davidson. So we sought the advice of our dealer advisory council to better analyze what we had to do.

Motor Accessories

In 1982, Harley-Davidson had a Motor Accessories catalog that was just 28 pages. Today, it's over 850. Motor Accessories makes up a significant portion of overall company revenue and profit.

We sent out product managers and engineers to bike rallies and observed all the choppers—bikes that had been modified by riders to reflect their individual tastes. We saw all this stuff that guys were buying for their Harleys, stuff that was not made by Harley-Davidson. We said, "Hey, we can make that. And those, we can make those, too. And that and that . . ."

Harley riders were mostly guys—back then, about 90 percent or more—and guys needed somewhere to ride on a Saturday afternoon while their wives were out shopping. We needed to give them a reason to cruise on over to their local Harley dealer.

We decided to focus on accessories, the accessories that guys could buy for their bikes for around $20—the chrome mirror, the license plate bracket, and the chrome covers—giving them a reason to go to their dealer on a Saturday.

Accessories had to be simple to install. We developed accessories that could be installed or removed in thirty seconds without a tool. We called them "detachables" and "parking lot items" because riders would install them in the parking lot with just a twist here or a snap there. Bike owners loved them, and the dealers quickly sold out and ordered more.

Once we had the products engineered and production readied, we set an objective to double the number of accessories we sold within three years and triple it in five; "2× in 3, 3× in 5" became a mantra around the company.

Our chief engineer said we were crazy. We didn't have enough people to design all the new accessories we wanted to offer. He was constantly putting out fires and didn't have time to scrutinize résumés and interview two hundred people in order to find thirty-five good engineers.

We put human resources to work on the problem. We asked them to take in résumés, review the candidates' qualifications, and then present only the best to the chief engineer for final interviews. All he had to do was pick the ones with passion and put them to work.

I believe that when hiring, it's always best to look for passion. If you hire people with passion, they will never think of it as work because they will always be doing what they love. That's what we did. And that's what we got—designers and engineers who loved motorcycles, rode, understood bikes, understood bikers, and had passion for what they did. They did brilliant work, and they are the first reason why Motor Accessories has been so successful.

There are others. I have to hand it to our vendors. We were asking a lot from them. They would need to increase their capacity—hire new people, add equipment, add more space, and incur more expense. It would strain their cash flow and increase their risk.

Some of them did not or could not buy into the vision of 2× in 3, 3× in 5. We spent time replacing them, but mostly we found our vendors not only willing to share our vision, but eager to ride the wave of growth we promised.

Motor Accessories was a success. Showroom traffic increased. Dealers reported that sales of accessories were way up, and visitors to their showrooms were ordering more bikes, too. Riders preferred buying accessories for their bikes that were guaranteed to fit—after all, they were designed and made by the same company that made their bikes. (If the accessories were outsourced, the suppliers had to meet the quality specifications developed by Harley.) Most importantly, the accessories carried the Harley-Davidson brand, a brand name they knew and trusted.

Fade to Black

Most Harley T-shirts are black. There's a reason. For many years, motorcycles used chain drive, and proper maintenance called for oiling the chain before a ride. The oil would spin off the chain sprocket and leave a stripe of oil up the back of the rider. On a black T-shirt, it didn't show as much. A white T-shirt, even after washing, would still show the signs of oil stains. But not black. Harleys now use a fiber belt drive that requires no maintenance for lubrication. But, keeping with tradition, the number-one selling T-shirt color is still black.

A word of advice: when you buy a black Harley T-shirt, wash it a few times till it starts to fade. Nothing looks more rookie than a brand-new, solid-black Harley T-shirt.

Harley-Davidson MotorClothes

Since 1911, Harley-Davidson has sold leather motorcycle jackets and gloves. The jackets are designed specifically for riding, with protective leather, wind-resistant collars, and lots of pockets for all the miscellaneous things you need to carry on a bike trip. But as recently as the early 1980s, there were fewer than a dozen different models to choose from.

In the 1950s, James Dean and Marlon Brando made T-shirts and black leather jackets look tough. It was a good biker look, and Harley sold a lot of T-shirts bearing the Harley-Davidson logo. But leather jackets, T-shirts, gloves, and a limited line of boots were about it.

The Marketing Problem

Product: Who will design the clothes? How many of each style? What sizes? What materials?

Place: Where will MotorClothes be sold? Do we limit sales to dealerships? Or should we also sell through department stores? Do we want to open stand-alone boutiques?

Price: How do we price the clothes? What will they cost to design, manufacture, store, and ship? Will the retail price be competitive?

Promotion: Do we advertise just to Harley owners? Or everybody? Where do we advertise? Should we use radio, TV, newspapers, magazines? Should we combine our advertising with dealerships?

In 1986, a call inquiring about licensing a line of Harley denims came in from Rome, Italy. The next month, a meeting and a tour of fifty clothing boutiques in Italy convinced me that the opportunity for Harley clothing was almost unlimited, with the right prices, designs, and marketing.

Every spring and fall, there is a big clothing show in Paris called the SEHM show, where over 3,000 vendors gather to display their new lines—not the high-fashion types, but regular clothiers like Gap, Brooks Brothers, Aéropostale, and Diesel. In the spring of 1987, I went there to search for a European distributor that would call on retailers and set them up with Harley-Davidson merchandise.

That show pointed up some of the problems we were having with our line of clothing. The designs from our T-shirt vendors were different from leather vendors, which were different from all our other vendors. There didn't seem to be any continuity from one design to the next.

So we talked about the design, distribution, and pricing issues and came to the conclusion that we should get serious about the clothing business: make all types of clothing and bring all the Harley clothing under one label. We hired a lead designer to coordinate all the vendor designers and licensed the name to manufacturers to provide a complete, unified line of clothing. The name: Harley-Davidson MotorClothes.

We developed a separate logo, not the black and orange of the motorcycle business, but tans and golds and earth tones. Very upscale looking, it used the symbol of an eagle with the inscription: "Harley-Davidson MotorClothes, an American Legend."

Our vision was head to toe, helmets to boots, and everything in between: belts, buckles, bags, caps, gloves, vests, bandanas, and chaps. Gear to keep you warm, gear to keep you dry, gear to keep you visible in the dark of night.

The vision didn't end there. We began to think beyond clothes. We wanted anything and everything that fit the Harley-Davidson rider profile: watches and jewelry, fragrances for both men and women, toys, cigarettes, and coffee (really strong coffee, naturally). We even offered furniture—leather couches and chairs emblazoned with the Bar and Shield. There were unusual big-ticket items to create interest in the dealers' showrooms: pool tables, jukeboxes, and old-fashioned Harley-Davidson pinball machines.

Dealers were scared to death. To be honest, so were we. This was not our core business. Harley-Davidson made motorcycles. What did we know about making clothes? Or coffee? Or furniture?

We needed clothing designers to create the look we wanted and choose the fabrics and materials. We needed vendors to construct the patterns and sew the garments. We needed new inventory control methods to keep track of the multitude of lines in a wide variety of sizes. We needed warehousing space to store everything. We needed a lot.

Our dealers had reasons of their own to worry about MotorClothes. What did they know about selling apparel? They sold bikes. They needed to hire and train a sales staff that knew and understood retail apparel. They needed to install clothes racks and mirrors, and to build dressing rooms and public bathrooms. Our dealers needed a lot, too.

All wisdom and logic said MotorClothes would fail. We plunged ahead anyway.

Extending the brand through MotorClothes was not without challenges. We solved many of the product problems by licensing our name and logo to a variety of vendors (more on that later). We told the clothing manufacturers what we wanted, and then we reviewed their designs, changing this, tweaking that. But mostly, we let them do what they did best—make apparel. They knew where to find the materials, how to lay out the patterns, and how to cut and sew the garments. We also outsourced the inventory and warehousing. The whole effort would have failed if not for the team that put it all together. A designer, a product manager, a purchasing manager, and an accountant all shared the same vision and developed the strategy to get there.

Part Numbers

In keeping with the motorcycle mentality, each article of clothing had a part number rather than style designation.

Most dealers didn't know anything about clothing—and didn't want to—so they would let their wives choose the apparel for their showrooms: "I'll take two of those and one of those, but I don't like that one, so we'll skip it. Oh, and I'll take that style, but only in size extra large." That just was not going to work.

In 1989, we introduced the MotorClothes concept and the leather jacket collection to the dealer network. We strongly encouraged dealers to take the complete MotorClothes package.

To encourage participation, we promised three things:

1. They didn't have to pay for the jackets for six months.

2. Every jacket that didn't sell at the end of one year could be returned for full credit.

3. Each package would come with a free merchandising display.

We had completely eliminated their risk. Still, while some enthusiastically embraced the program—they recognized that MotorClothes could be a new profit center for them—others seemed unconvinced. In that first year, just 232 out of our 620 dealers signed up for the complete package.

Cycle King

Harley-Davidson was the first company to use silicon injection to make three-dimensional jackets. The vendor created a 3-D logo in leather. Harley called the jacket "Cycle King." It became the company's biggest seller.

I was disappointed. At our next big dealer convention, with one year of MotorClothes sales behind us, I made my presentation—a colorful slide show that talked about all the new MotorClothes and all the new programs and services. Then I wrapped up my comments by simply saying, "This past year, we sold over 6,000 Cycle King jackets, and I want to thank those 232 dealers who ordered them." That was it, nothing else about leather jackets. I remember watching the faces of the other dealers. Many looked shocked—"Boy, did we miss out on something."

The phones began to ring. Dealers called in to sign up for the program. That next year, we doubled sales of Cycle King jackets. We also had nearly 100 percent dealer participation.

The late 1980s were the growth years for Harley. The demand for bikes exceeded the supply, and the waiting list for new bikes stretched out for well over a year; showroom floors became almost empty. The MotorClothes team filled the space with new products, new displays, and new opportunities to make money and upgrade the brand image.

What Size?

If you think it's tough to design a motorcycle that reflects the rugged individualism of our target market, try clothes. Fickle, fickle, fickle. And sizes? People of all sizes and shapes ride Harley-Davidson motorcycles. *All* sizes and shapes.

One year in Daytona, a huge rider came up to me and poked his finger in my chest. He was a cop from Queens and weighed easily 300 pounds. He wanted to know why Harley didn't make jackets to fit guys his size.

"We will next year," I said. (As a general rule, it's wise not to argue with a cop, especially one much bigger than you.)

When I got back to Milwaukee, we added XXL and XXXL to our complete clothing line.

The next year, the Queens cop found me at Daytona, proudly wearing his XXXL Harley jacket.

Licensing

The buyout in 1981 could not have been worse for timing. The Japanese were dumping product on the market. Interest rates were at a lofty 18 percent. Gas prices were at record highs, and gas was scarce; lines at gas stations often stretched around the block. Motorcycle sales plummeted, and Harley began hemorrhaging money.

The company lost almost $20 million that first full year of independence. Just to prove it was no fluke, we followed that by losing a whopping $30 million the second year. Production went from 48,000 bikes in 1980 to just over 30,000 in 1982. Harley laid off 40 percent of its workforce; 1,600 people lost their jobs. The 2,200 who remained took a 10 percent pay cut, and all 401(k) funding was suspended.

Harley needed cash, fast. That meant sales. But where were the sales going to come from? I called together our marketing team, and we came up with a list of ways to build the business:

- Sponsor and promote rock concerts
- Make the racing team a profit center
- Create a motorcycle club
- License the Harley name

The last two were the first to be approved for a couple of reasons. Forming a motorcycle club wouldn't cost much, and it added value to a buyer's purchase. It also encouraged more riders and more riding, which would likely lead to more sales. (For more on the motorcycle club, see chapter 1.) Licensing would cost next to nothing, and it meant immediate cash to a company in desperate need for cash.

Paperwork a Problem, Licensing the Solution

I met with one of our product managers and saw papers strewn all over his desk, on the floor, everywhere. Some stacks were over a foot high.

When I asked, he told me that they were invoices for T-shirts. All of them. Some for as little as a few dollars, some for thousands.

We were a company bleeding cash, and we couldn't keep up with the paperwork. We needed to find someone else to take over the problem.

When we began to license our trademark and logo to others, the paperwork became *their* problem. We simply collected a royalty on everything they sold.

Prior to the buyout, AMF had done virtually nothing to protect the Harley-Davidson brand. In 1986, there were 490 companies using the Harley-Davidson name or logo without our permission. Some of the bootleggers were abusing our name—producing T-shirts with obscene, racist, or drug-related messages that clearly did not serve to enhance the Harley image.

In order to regain control of the brand, Harley's corporate attorney chose one of the worst offenders, Joe's MCN, a company that made drug paraphernalia brandishing the Harley Bar and Shield, and filed suit. We won.

We immediately mailed out 489 cease-and-desist letters. It took a while to shut down all the infringers; some required legal action, others a personal visit. Our legal department also began a comprehensive effort to register five different trademarks in thirteen different classes. The same had to be done in Europe.

Harley-Davidson knew nothing about licensing. Clearly, selling T-shirts, coffee mugs, boots, or the myriad other products we thought we could make money on was not our core competency. So we asked questions and got sound advice from a number of outside experts, including the McDonald's® restaurant chain's director of retail marketing. He gave us two valuable bits of advice. First, do it right; licensing can be very lucrative. Second, watch out for the shady people out there; you could get burned. We did some homework and found a New York firm that specialized in licensing to the toy industry, and they taught us the business.

Then we began traveling around the country and meeting with the largest producers of unlicensed products, evaluating them and signing up the best with contracts. Our pitch went something like this:

> A license agreement with Harley-Davidson® is an opportunity like no other. With over 95 percent consumer recognition, we are going to make it one of the most powerful brands in the world. The legendary Bar and Shield™ has been the launching point for a diverse line of Harley-Davidson products and services ranging from T-shirts to bicycles, leather wallets to collectible dolls, eyewear to cafés. As our licensing program grows, so will the rewards. Care to join us?

We had to rely on a cadre of manufacturers. Unfortunately, not all could be trusted. Heck, many had been using our name and logo without our permission for years. Some had distribution deals on the side. For instance, they would sell to distributors that they owned, which then sold to a wholesaler (which they also may have owned), which then sold to the retailer. Royalties were paid based on the wholesale price. So they managed to steal a little more profit at each selling point in the distribution channel. We made a few mistakes like that till we learned their tricks.

Ultimately, we negotiated legal contracts using a few simple principles:

- **Term of contract**—Length of the license term varied by category, dependent upon the up-front costs (for example, tooling) and type of product (for example, novelties had a short lifespan).

- **Royalty rate**—These differed by category but were based on the wholesale price (not including returns or warranties) and were paid either monthly or quarterly.

- **The property**—This referred to which specific logo or trademark was to be used on a specific product.

- **Renewal date**—This depended on tooling and/or testing requirements, the investment assumed by the manufacturer—the more the investment required, the longer the term.

- **Advance**—A minimum payment was required up front as an advance on royalties, which served as an incentive for the company to recoup its investment sooner.

- **Minimum guarantee**—This was an annual minimum dollar amount, but we also required a minimum over the length of the contract.

- **Territory**—Most companies wanted the world, but the contract was usually limited to areas of distribution they already covered with their other products—state, region, country, continent.

- **Distribution**—This clause controlled who the licensee could sell to—we didn't want to be in discount stores like Wal-Mart or Target—to maintain an upscale image. Harley dealers frequently enjoyed exclusive distribution and retail rights.

- **Scope of the license**—This specified the product and its content to ensure quality (for example, T-shirts had to be 100 percent cotton with a minimum thread count).

- **Exclusivity**—This referred to whether the licensee was the only one who would be making the product.

- **Key employee clause**—We preferred to deal with people, not companies, so we used a key employee clause—if the principal left, died, retired, or was otherwise no longer involved, the contract became void.

- **Arbitration**—This was the only legal remedy for any disputes; we wanted to avoid expensive lawsuits.

Sales from licensing agreements reached nearly $1 million that first year, a godsend for a company bleeding cash. By 1987, revenues were over $2 million and grew steadily thereafter.

Harley-Davidson Licensing Revenues

1987: $2,327,000	1991: $6,709,000
1988: $3,868,000	1992: $9,564,000
1989: $5,420,000	2010: $37,000,000
1990: $5,317,000*	

* We canceled a large T-shirt licensee that was sending us royalty payments of a million dollars a year but distributing shirts in places that did not enhance the brand.

The vast array of products enhanced the Harley image across a wide variety of audiences. L'Oréal perfumes and colognes gave Harley-Davidson cachet. Bulova watches gave Harley-Davidson prestige. Ford F-150 co-branding enhanced Harley-Davidson's image of rugged dependability. Designer Nicole Miller made Harley-Davidson hip and trendy with silk clothing items that were sold in leading department stores like Bloomingdale's.

T-shirts became our biggest success. By eliminating fifty-fifty poly-cotton blends and increasing the thread count, we were licensing only high-quality shirts. We were also able to eliminate crude graphics and offensive language.

Harley-Davidson Hot Wheels™ were also a big success. For several years, we sold more toy riding motorcycles than real riding motorcycles. Could the kids playing with Hot Wheels motorcycles be future riders?

Fragrances had mixed results. Harley-Davidson Legends aftershave and cologne from L'Oréal were big sellers in Russia for several years. But in Europe, they were sold in midrange retail outlets rather than at high-end retailers exclusively. It cheapened the perceived value of the fragrances, and they never sold as well as they could have.

We quickly learned that selling denims at Bloomingdale's, J. C. Penney, and Sears angered the dealer network. They feared what might be next—motorcycles?

Our biggest mistake was to license cigarettes to Lorillard. At the time, smoking was an acceptable practice. Cigarettes seemed like a natural extension of the rugged individualism sought by the average biker. Times changed, and we eventually negotiated out of the contract.

Biker Brew

Coffee is a novelty item, but we licensed it because it fit the Harley lifestyle. It was a tradition for riders to stop off at their local dealership for a cup of coffee when out on a Saturday ride. Harley used it as a "smile" item, not a serious money maker. Copy on the packaging reads:

> In the mid 1950s, Harley rider "Panhead" Valdez took a wrong turn in El Paso, Texas, and ended up in Central America. During his extended stay, his distant cousin, Juan, woke him up one day at noon with a uniquely distinctive aroma steaming from a pot of fresh brewed coffee. It was reported that the beans for this coffee were picked by the virgin daughters of the local townspeople by the light of the full moon.

> Having heard this tale at a gaming table in Deadwood, South Dakota, during the 50th Black Hills Classic, fellow Hog member and coffer blender Tom Charleville set out to rediscover this brew. After scouring the hills and mountains of Central and South America for many, many moons, he is now pleased to present you with this "Bikers Brew."

> All we ask is that each morning, when preparing this Harley-Davidson custom blend of coffee, you take a few moments of silence to reflect on the passing of "Panhead" and his pickers.

Successes far outnumbered the missteps. For instance, at one time, Harley was selling 4,000 pairs of boots a year without a license agreement. Imagine Harley-Davidson, that renowned manufacturer of heavyweight motorcycles, buying boots and reselling them. It was crazy. We were not in the footwear business. We were buried in inventory problems and paperwork. Something had to change, and it did. We talked with boot makers, visited some factories, shook some hands, and eventually negotiated a licensing agreement that resulted in sales of over a million boots a year.

Licensing is almost all profit. Choose a quality manufacturer, a good business partner, and approve the designs. Specify the quality. Monitor sales. Collect the royalties. About 90 percent goes to the bottom line.

If Harley could license the name and logo, could the distinctive sound made by a Harley-Davidson V-twin engine also be licensed?

I was at a toy expo to investigate licensing opportunities when I stumbled upon a manufacturer who had designed a toy that contained a computer chip capable of mimicking the familiar "potato, potato, potato" sound of a Harley V-twin engine.

This alarmed me. Somebody could make a toy motorcycle that sounded like a Harley, and we would have no control over the use of that unique sound. I asked our legal department to look into trademarking the Harley sound. It was an interesting concept. Music can be copyrighted. NBC's three-note (G-E-C) sign-off is trademarked. So is the roar of MGM's lion.

> ## Harley-Davidson Trademark Licensing
>
> In the early 1990s, licensing brought in a significant amount of revenue. In terms of the number of licenses sold, the biggest sellers fell into four categories: clothing, children's, novelties, and foreign. In just one year, these categories made up 70 percent of the trademark licenses sold and amounted to nearly ten million dollars. The remaining 30 percent were distributed among the following categories:
>
> * Leather accessories
> * Jewelry accessories
> * Other accessories
> * Specialties
> * Gifts/collectibles

Harley filed for a trademark but eventually decided the legal fees were not in the budget. Some of the publicity surrounding the effort was negative, but the point had been made. The sound of a Harley is indeed unique. The Japanese companies couldn't claim that about their bikes.

Brand Extension in Europe

In 1986, on a trip to Italy to call on some dealers, I had a chance to visit Energy, a fashion boutique in Rome. Run by a Moroccan named Philipe, Energy had the unique distinction of being a trendsetter in European street fashion.

Its windows attracted fashionistas throughout Europe. One window display, for instance, used live monkeys that simply tossed fashionable attire into the air while passersby watched—that is, until animal cruelty people protested, and Philipe was forced to change the display. The windows were taped over for weeks. When the store reopened, it made headlines throughout the continent. In a king-size bed were what appeared to be two naked women and a single naked man (hidden discreetly beneath bed sheets), their chic clothing stylishly strewn about the floor.

I immediately liked Philipe's showmanship. We talked over espresso one afternoon, and I asked him what he thought might be the next big trend in fashion. When he suggested American-style motorcycle wear, we worked out a deal, and I shipped him dozens of leather jackets, T-shirts, bandanas, and two Harley-Davidson motorcycles for a window display. His next window treatment helped launch MotorClothes throughout Europe.

But we soon discovered a problem. Despite all the hype and the display at Energy, the jackets didn't sell as well as we had hoped. After a quick look at the numbers, we discovered that a jacket that sold for $400 in the United States was selling for $850 or more in Europe.

Or rather, it wasn't selling. Too pricey. By the time we brought it into the States from Indonesia or Korea or wherever it was being made, paid the import duties, added warehousing costs, shipped it to Europe, and paid some more import duties and warehousing costs, the leathers were just too expensive for the average person.

One of the vendors that made leather jackets for the US market asked for a license to sell leathers in Europe as well. But the vendor didn't want to sell the *same* leather jackets, vests, and pants that we were selling in the United States. Those were made to be worn while riding. This vendor had an idea to produce a completely new line of biker clothing, not for riding, but for styling, spending a night on the town. The company wanted to make biker wear to be worn as street fashion.

> "Every new product introduction is like a new flowering plant. At first it weeps, then it creeps, then it leaps."
>
> —Harley proverb

The vendor also pointed out a major difference between the US market and the European market. Simply put, a Harley jacket didn't fit the European physique. Americans, it seems, have longer arms and are generally heavier. Jackets designed for the American market were about two or three inches too long in the sleeves and about two or three inches too wide in the waistline for Europeans.

This led to a whole new line of MotorClothes. Our designers instructed vendors to make a completely different set of sizes for the European market. We also made major changes in styling. Some fashion jackets were made of lambskin and never could have withstood the rigors of the road.

Pricing issues were resolved, too. Many of the denims and some of the leather goods were made in Europe, avoiding much of the shipping costs and all the import duties. Prices were soon in line with similar goods made by competitors.

That's when the new line leapt. Sales skyrocketed throughout Europe. Riding wear soon became popular among the fashion elite. Motorcycle clothing became haute couture in Milan and Paris. The biker look was in, very hip, très trendy. No longer just for riders, it was a look that everybody seemed to want. People wore it everywhere. Movie stars and politicians proudly wore Harley-Davidson MotorClothes. Rock stars sported Harley gear on stage in front of thousands of fans. Harley became a fashion statement. By 1992, we were winning fashion awards. For instance, on February 5, 1992, Harley-Davidson received an award from the Council of Fashion Designers of America for bringing Harley-Davidson MotorClothes into the mainstream of fashion.

It was a huge success. Sales of Harley-Davidson MotorClothes almost equaled those of Motor Accessories. MotorClothes accounted for nearly $50 million by 1992.

Brand Extension in the States

To kick-start Harley-Davidson MotorClothes in the United States, we initiated a trade-in program: bring any leather jacket (not just a Harley jacket) into your Harley dealer and receive a certificate good for $100 off the purchase of any new Harley jacket.

Here's how it worked: The dealer gave the customer a $100 discount for each jacket they traded in on a new jacket. Harley-Davidson bought it from the dealer for $50 then sold the jackets to a secondhand store for $25 each. So the program cost us $25 per jacket, and it cost the dealers $50 per jacket.

It was a bonanza. Stores were flooded with customers, and Harley jackets flew off the shelves. Best of all, many of the buyers were new to the Harley brand. That was great news. We figured if you wore the MotorClothes, you might one day own a bike. Many people today are first introduced to Harley-Davidson through MotorClothes—a Harley jacket or T-shirt. Clothing serves as an introduction to the rider aura, the biker mystique. Most importantly, the logo wear identifies you as a rugged individual, the personification of the Harley-Davidson brand.

The Marketing Solution

Product: We found designers to create the clothing to our specifications. We made them all exclusively of leather that first year. We shipped packages (not individual jackets) of six sizes in twelve styles. Each one had a part number—not just a name or size designation, but a part number.

Place: We sold exclusively through Harley dealerships at first. Later, we also sold through boutiques and stand-alone stores owned by Harley dealers. We encouraged dealers to call us each Monday morning to reorder any clothing sold during the weekend so that they always had a full package in stock.

Price: We priced MotorClothes at a 20 percent premium over similar apparel without the Harley-Davidson logo. We sold packages to dealers so their markup would give them a 50 percent profit margin. If they reordered individual garments, they would receive a 35 percent margin.

Promotion: We created MotorClothes brochures using gritty black-and-white photography, and we ran similar gritty-looking ads in motorcycle magazines. In addition, we gave a jacket to nearly every rock 'n' roll star that came through Milwaukee. Many wore their leather either on stage or during interviews in front of the cameras.

We soon opened a few fashion boutiques in high-traffic areas—airports and tourist-rich venues. Our first stand-alone store was in the Royal Hawaiian Shopping Center in Honolulu. Other boutiques followed. Some dealers complained about the competition—boutiques selling the same Harley MotorClothes they offered—so we agreed to set up each boutique store with the dealership in that territory. Many dealers now operate both bike stores and boutiques; the boutiques serve as feeders for their bike stores.

MotorClothes Sales

1986	1990	2010
$20M	$125M	$258M

Dealers appreciated the added traffic that MotorClothes sent to their showrooms. New customers, people who might have never walked through their doors, came in to shop for fashion clothing, leather jackets, bandanas, and other Harley logo wear. While browsing the showrooms, they could look at those shiny motorcycles with a hint of wonder in their eyes: "Could this be for me?"

As MotorClothes grew, other products followed: jewelry, watches and clocks, piggy (hog) banks, cups and mugs, toys, sunglasses, coffee, and beer (Harley Heavy). All carried the Harley-Davidson name, a trusted brand.

Brand Extension Down Under

At Harley, there is a popular saying: "If you want to change something, measure it." I applied that thinking to a detailed year-end international sales report in 1990 and discovered that, even though we sold about 3,000 bikes a year in Australia, sales of MotorClothes and Motor Accessories were almost nonexistent.

I soon discovered that we had the same pricing problems in Australia that we had had in Europe; the import duties, shipping and handling costs, plus the distributors' markup made a $400 leather jacket jump to over $800 at retail in Sydney. Similar pricing applied to boots, leather goods, T-shirts, and a variety of other goods that appealed to Harley riders.

We concluded that we would need to hire local manufacturers if we wanted to sell more MotorClothes in Australia and New Zealand. I researched manufacturers there and found several that could produce Harley merchandise to our quality standards. Of course, I wanted to meet them—inspect their facilities, examine their quality standards, shake some hands, look them in the eye. They were to be our business partners, and we needed to know we could trust them. The time was right for a trip down under.

Now, at that same time, there was an Australian motorcycle parts distributor called All Harley Imports. They were anything but. They had a 400-page catalog that featured Harley accessories, but in fact, they were all just aftermarket parts simply made to fit Harley motorcycles. We hired some Australian attorneys and sent the company numerous cease-and-desist letters, but they were all ignored. Both our legal bills and our dealer complaints were mounting.

I called the president of All Harley Imports and told him that I was flying over to meet him. He was astonished to think that I would come all the way from Milwaukee to settle legal issues with a small operator like All Harley Imports. I told him the $8,000 cost to fly there was a lot less than the cost to sue him. He accepted the meeting.

An Australian trademark consultant set up my appointment schedule:

Week one—Monday to Thursday, meet with potential manufacturers and present the program

Week one—Friday, meet with All Harley Imports

Week one—Saturday and Sunday, meet with Harley distributors and together select manufacturers in each category

Week two—Monday through Friday, sign up the new manufacturers as licensees

Week two—Saturday and Sunday, ride

When we signed up the Australian and New Zealand manufacturers, we arranged for our US producers to send their designs, graphics, patterns, and specifications—even the type of buttons and zippers—so our customers could always feel they were getting the real thing and would wear it proudly.

Not all of the new manufacturers were big companies. Tony Blaine, owner of Acme Products, printed T-shirts in his garage; a parachute hung from the ceiling to prevent paint chips from dropping on his inventory. Tony and his one employee (his wife) were good people who wanted to succeed, and I knew they would be easy to work with. After he signed a license agreement with us, his business really took off. Acme even became the official licensee for the Sydney Olympics and produced all the T-shirts bearing the Olympics logo. Some years later, Tony sold Acme Products—his 200-plus employees were sad to see him go—to start an antique motorcycle store, where he found a home for his collection of twenty-five Harleys.

The meeting with All Harley Imports also went well. The owner picked me up at the Adelaide airport and drove me to his home, which was located in the back of the shop. His wife made egg salad sandwiches, and we sat around the kitchen table to strike a deal. He agreed to destroy all his catalogs and any promotional materials that suggested he sold original Harley-Davidson parts. I agreed to pay him $800 to tear down his sign and replace it with something that did not refer to Harley-Davidson. It was a win-win. And the egg salad was delicious.

By 1994, we had nine manufacturers supplying just the Australian and New Zealand market, selling everything from leather jackets and footwear to novelties and over 10,000 Harley-Davidson T-shirts a month.

Australia and New Zealand are half a world away from Milwaukee. It represented a huge risk, yes. But if you don't take any risk, you can face unknowable losses. The key in conducting business on an international basis is: find people with the same values and make them your partners.

Overextended

By the 1990s, our dealership network had changed. No longer could a dealer simply be a good mechanic able to plug the oil pan on a leaky Shovelhead or smooth the stroke of a stubborn V-twin. Now he had to be a businessman. A dealer had to be able to manage multiple inventories of bikes, accessories, and apparel. He had to be able to train new bikers, if he had a Rider's Edge program. He had to be able to hire and train a sales staff that could talk fashion, not just Fat Boy. He had to be able to understand credit, financing, and future value tables. He had to think smarter, because he had more opportunities to fail.

But he also had many additional opportunities to make a lot more money. Harley-Davidson created complete packages across a broad range of products and services, with pricing that offered dealers significant opportunities to increase their turnovers, better their margins, and make a better profit:

- Motorcycles
- Rider training
- Motorcycle insurance
- Motorcycle financing (45 percent of all Harleys sold)
- Motor Accessories
- MotorClothes
- Motorcycle service

In our efforts to extend the Harley-Davidson name and image worldwide, lots of mistakes were made, such as L'Oréal's positioning of personal care products in drugstores in Europe. Nothing ever goes as smoothly as you hope it will. But we always managed to solve the problems following two primary principles. First, we made it easy to do business with Harley-Davidson. We kept everything as simple as we could. We wanted our partners to make money, too. Second, we chose to work with companies we could trust. If they had the same goals and values as we did in Milwaukee, they became our partners.

Traditionalists scoff at the "Disneyfication" of the storied name. But Harley believes that brand extension meets the needs of existing customers who want to identify with Harley-Davidson even when they're not riding one—to demonstrate their rugged individualism, to express their lifestyle, to be admired for the Harley look.

Brand extension also serves to reach out to new customers. Buy the kid a bicycle that looks like a Harley; dress the baby in clothes sporting the Bar and Shield; and get the Harley-Davidson leather jacket and riding gloves for yourself, even if you don't own a bike. Yet.

3

BRAND ASSOCIATION

Imagine: You are out for an evening of entertainment. You decide to combine your love of rock 'n' roll with the social aspects of drinking and dining with friends.

At the Hard Rock Cafe, the noise and energy slam you like a fist as you enter. Everywhere are the memorabilia of the most-celebrated, the most-revered rock 'n' roll stars who have ever plucked a Fender Stratocaster® or beat a Zildjian cymbal to ear-popping limits. You are in awe of the gold records on the walls (Hendrix and The Who), the autographed guitars (Clapton, Winters, Simmons), and a pair of crossed drumsticks signed by Ginger Baker.

The music of these rock 'n' roll gods batters your ears; you know you'll wake in the morning with your ears still ringing. Your body begins to move with the backbeat rhythms. Your feet tap, even stomp, along with the drumming. The smell of fried food and old beer mingles with the perspiration and heavy breathing of a hundred other people doing exactly the same thing.

And there, amid this cacophony of noise and sweat and pure unadulterated joy, right there in the middle of the lobby, spotlights dancing off its gleaming chrome, sits a big, beautiful, shiny Harley-Davidson motorcycle.

And all is right and good in your world.

You are a rock 'n' roll junkie. You enjoy the music, and you naturally enjoy those things associated with the music—the good times, the food, socializing with friends, and Harley-Davidson motorcycles. It is brand association at its most effective.

What Is Brand Association?

Brand association is a promotional technique as old as marketing itself. Create an image for an unknown brand based upon its association with a known commodity: a person, a smell, a sound, a place, or a thing, something or someone that your target audience knows and understands. Use the known commodity to create an impression that your product or service has the same qualities or characteristics that make that commodity special or unique. The association conjures up thoughts, feelings, images, experiences, beliefs, attitudes, and so on, which become linked to that brand.

> ### Rugged Individualism
>
> Harley-Davidson is not the only company to associate its brand with rugged individualism.
>
> Launched in 1924, Marlboro was marketed as a cigarette for ladies. Its advertising campaign, "Mild as May," focused on attracting women to the brand.
>
> In the 1950s, Chicago ad agency Leo Burnett repositioned Marlboro using a cowboy to represent the brand as a manly cigarette. In less than a year, the brand's market share rose from less than 1 percent to fourth best-selling brand. Today, it ranks first worldwide.

The goal is to develop or align expectations. You create an expectation for the brand when it is associated with a known commodity. The brand has certain qualities or characteristics that make it special or unique; the commodity causes you to recall that which is special or unique.

Brand association begins with the commodity—the person, place, product, sound, or smell—you wish to associate with your brand. There are many vehicles you can use to create a brand association, such as:

- Celebrity
- Authority
- Symbol
- Event
- Charity
- Mnemonic

A celebrity endorsement associates a brand with someone famous. Choosing a celebrity who appeals to a similar target market as your product or service exposes your brand to prospective customers. Choose wisely. If a celebrity endorses too many products, it can dilute the recall value of your product. Or if your celebrity suddenly goes crazy or does something that loses his or her fan base (à la Charlie Sheen or Tiger Woods), you can too.

A third-party authority can build credibility for your brand, which is especially helpful when introducing a new product. When Procter & Gamble first obtained the American Dental Association endorsement for Crest® toothpaste, it boosted a small player in the toothpaste category to number one. Fifty years later, the competition still hasn't caught up.

A symbol—a logo, a critter, or a signature—can identify a brand. Quick, what comes to mind when you see Tony the Tiger or golden arches?

Event sponsorship can associate a brand with an event—Budweiser and the Olympics, Miller beer and a Milwaukee Brewers baseball game—and create goodwill among event goers. Harley-Davidson's sponsorship of rallies throughout the world has brought the brand closer to its customers and its customers closer to the brand.

Getting involved in a charity offers many advantages for a brand. People like to work with other people who care about their community. It's important to choose a charitable organization that fits your company profile and aligns your brand with the organization's membership. Harley-Davidson examined many different options before choosing to align itself with the Muscular Dystrophy Association (more on this in chapter 5).

Advertisers often use a mnemonic device, a memory trigger, to recall a brand. Sometimes it is a tagline ("Fly the friendly skies" or "Nothing runs like a Deere"), a critter (Tony the Tiger or the Jolly Green Giant), or a jingle.

Co-Branding

Co-branding refers to two (or more) companies cooperating to combine the strengths of both brands in order to increase the premium consumers are willing to pay. When an airline cooperates with a credit card company to offer mileage for each purchase, that's co-branding. When a cake mix company uses a chocolate company's morsels in its package, that's co-branding. When the Ford F-150 added black leather interior and distinct Harley styling, that was co-branding.

Best Western® runs an exclusive rewards program for members of HOG. Riders who participate get special treatment at the hotel, including a clean wipe-down towel at check-in. This program benefits both Best Western, by encouraging riders to stay at Best Western inns, and Harley-Davidson, by creating an added benefit for HOG members.

The primary benefit of co-branding is the decrease in the cost of brand positioning. Millions are spent creating an image for a brand. Combined with the millions spent by another brand, that's millions and millions that contribute to the positioning of both brands. Another win-win.

Brand Association in Film

Product placement is another type of brand association. One of the most successful examples of motion picture product placement, Reese's Pieces® in *E.T.: The Extra-Terrestrial*, associated a relatively new product with one of the most popular movies of all time. When Mars declined his offer to use M&M's®, Producer Steven Spielberg approached the Hershey Company and its Reese's Pieces.[6]

Reese's Pieces—a brand extension of Reese's Peanut Butter Cups—was first introduced in 1980. Outspent by M&M's, its sales sagged. In a bold move, Hershey agreed to spend $1 million on advertising during the movie's release in return for being allowed to use *E.T.* to promote Reese's Pieces. The movie was released in June 1982 and was an immediate hit. Within two weeks, sales of Reese's Pieces tripled. Distributors couldn't keep the retailers stocked.

Today, Reese's Pieces is a leader in the candy market, outselling its parent peanut butter cups nearly two to one. It is estimated that Hershey paid $1 million for exposure worth $15–20 million.

The kind of exposure Harley got in *Hells Angels on Wheels* was brand association at its worst. This association was further emphasized with the 1991 movie *Harley Davidson and the Marlboro Man* starring Mickey Rourke and Don Johnson as, you guessed it, roughnecks and hooligans. These motion pictures reinforced the negative image of riders as packs of lawless renegades, a stereotype the company still actively strives to dispel.

A more recent motion picture featuring Harley-Davidson motorcycles is Walt Disney's *Wild Hogs* (2007). In it, John Travolta, Tim Allen, Martin Lawrence, and William H. Macy portray a group of middle-aged suburbanites suffering through midlife crises. They take a road trip on their Harleys to get away from their unadventurous home lives and experience the thrill of the open road. While some might argue that Disney and Harley-Davidson don't mix (*Wild Hogs* received tepid reviews), the picture serves as a departure from previous depictions of Harley riders.

Rock 'N' Roll

What better association could a brand ask for than rock 'n' roll? I mean, it's everywhere. It permeates our everyday lives—on radio, television, and digital media players; in our homes, our cars, restaurants, elevators, and waiting rooms.

Everyone likes it, or at least some of it. Many companies have tried to associate themselves with various groups or individuals. But over the years, I don't think any company has created better brand association with rock 'n' roll music and individual rock 'n' roll icons than Harley-Davidson.

Who Is God?

It was my policy to give a leather jacket to rock 'n' roll stars who came through Milwaukee. I felt it was great exposure and a legitimate promotion. But jackets were expensive, and every one given away had to be approved by a senior officer.

Jeff Bluestein, president at the time, came up to me in the hallway at a dealer advisory council meeting with a requisition slip in his hand. He asked me, "Who is this guy 'E. Clapton' that you want to give a jacket to?"

Coincidentally, one of our biggest dealers was walking down that same hallway at the time. So I called out to him, "Hey, Oliver. Who is God?"

He said, "Eric Clapton."

Bluestein signed it.

Back in the 1960s, Isaac Tigrett and Peter Morton founded the Hard Rock Cafe. The restaurants combined rock 'n' roll music, memorabilia related to rock 'n' roll, and traditional American cuisine. They were an immediate success, and by the early 1980s, there were dozens of Hard Rock Cafes around the world.

I first met with Isaac in 1986 in Dallas. He was a smart businessman, and we quickly struck an agreement to place Harley-Davidson

Softails in several Hard Rock Cafes on the East Coast. We also explored the possibility of putting the Hard Rock Cafe logo on a special-edition Harley-Davidson bike in exchange for the right to display a Harley in every Hard Rock Cafe throughout the world. This was to be the first time Harley would put a logo other than its own on a motorcycle since the AMF days. Harley shipped bikes to Isaac's key restaurants, where they were prominently displayed to much oohing and aahing.

But Isaac owned only the Hard Rock Cafes east of the Mississippi. His partner, Peter Morton, controlled all the restaurants in the west. So I flew to Los Angeles to meet with Peter to discuss the deal with him. Waiting outside his office, I observed a brand-new Lamborghini in his parking space and the fancy trimmings in his reception area.

We had a cordial meeting. I explained the program that Isaac and I had agreed to, which included our supplying movie star Dan Aykroyd with the first Hard Rock Harley to promote the program.

Peter asked for a free special-edition bike to seal the deal. I replied, "No, you have to buy your first bike. We'll make you a deal on the second bike. But the first one is on you. We want you to join the family."

Peter figured if Aykroyd got one, he should get one, too. A free bike to Dan Aykroyd made business sense; Aykroyd riding a Harley was good publicity. But Peter Morton? The general public didn't know who he was. I wanted Peter to buy into the Harley mystique—he could certainly afford it—so I dug in my heels.

To this day, I have a gas tank bearing the Hard Rock Cafe logo that sits in my office as a reminder of the missed opportunity. By the late 1980s, the Hard Rock Cafe chain began to lose some of its edginess, and Isaac sold his interests to the Rank Organisation in 1990.

While the Hard Rock Cafe special-edition motorcycle never materialized, Harley-Davidson had immense success associating with bands and individual musicians. Music offers a wide variety of demographic and psychographic choices. Bands have their followings. Many choose to further their bad-boy images under the mantle of rugged individualism—the perfect audience for Harley.

Whenever the Doobie Brothers were appearing in the Wisconsin area, we would get a call in Milwaukee for motorcycles. Harley would ship them to wherever they were performing, and then they would ride into the next show on the bikes. Word spread. Other performers who were riders began to call us when they were in the area, too—Craig Chaquico, former lead guitarist for Jefferson Starship; Mark Knopfler of Dire Straits; Eric Clapton; and more. It was the perfect brand association, and it boosted both credibility and sales.

The World's Largest Music Festival

Summerfest is an annual music festival held on seventy acres along Milwaukee's lakefront. Over its ten days, the festival draws nearly a million people each year. According to the *Guinness Book of World Records* of 1999, it is the largest music festival in the world.

Rock 'N' Harley

The day after a helicopter crash in Wisconsin killed Stevie Ray Vaughan and members of Eric Clapton's crew, the *Chicago Tribune* showed a photograph of the wreckage. Clearly visible was Vaughan's Harley-Davidson denim jacket.

The main stage has seating for over 23,000, but ten other stages, sponsored by area businesses, offer informal seating areas for 7,000 to 10,000. The festival is a frequent venue for many rock 'n' roll legends as well as legends in the making.

In 1985, when the Pabst Brewing Company was sold and the company dropped its sponsorship of one of the Summerfest stages, the Milwaukee World Festival (the nonprofit organization that runs Summerfest) asked Harley-Davidson to step in. We had no money in the budget for something like this—the soundstage needed to be completely remodeled, new signage created, better seating installed, a beverage tent constructed. So we partnered with Miller Brewing (who already had its own stage) during that first year. Miller put up half the sponsorship money and built the beverage tent, for which they received all the beer vending rights. We, in turn, focused our funds on remodeling the facility. We named it the Harley-Davidson Roadhouse.

The Harley-Davidson Roadhouse became a big part of the World's Largest Music Festival. Each night of Summerfest, the Roadhouse featured a different theme—Hispanic music, reggae, African American, young, old, highbrow, or lowbrow—a diverse mix of musical tastes to attract a diverse crowd. Over the years, the Harley-Davidson Roadhouse has seen some of rock 'n' roll's greatest stars perform. The performers have one thing in common: they each appeal to an audience that could be interested in riding motorcycles. The Harley-Davidson Roadhouse was just one more opportunity for Harley to associate its brand with a rock 'n' roll performer's popularity and audience.

The Harley Racing Team

Founded in 1903, Harley-Davidson was one of the first companies to manufacture motorcycles. But by 1911, more than 150 other companies had entered the marketplace.

Breaking the 100 mph Barrier

In 1921, a motorcycle won a race with an average speed of more than 100 mph for the first time in history. That motorcycle was a Harley-Davidson.

Racing was one way to differentiate one bike company from another. Over the past century, Harley has enjoyed more than its share of winners.

In 1908, Walter Davidson, president and cofounder of Harley-Davidson, rode a single-cylinder motorcycle in an endurance race over New York's Catskill Mountains. Sixty-five bikers competed in the grueling two-day, 365-mile event. Davidson won, earning the only perfect score.

During the 1930s, Joe Petrali dominated the sport on Harley-Davidson motorcycles. After the war, Harley continued to dominate, winning nineteen of the twenty-three national events in 1948 and nineteen of twenty-four races in 1949. From 1953 through 1969, Harley-Davidson won thirteen times at the prestigious Daytona International Speedway. But after 1969, Harley's road-racing program struggled as the company went through a period of financial uncertainty. Harley could no longer support a road-racing team (though it did continue to support a dirt-track team).

The company faced a variety of difficulties in the 1980s, and despite the value a winning race team might add to the brand's image, we just didn't have the time or the dollars to make it work. Simply remaining solvent was our first priority.

That didn't mean we had forgotten our commitment to racing or didn't want to pursue it. It simply meant that, if we did, we had to find a way to make it part of our return to profitability. And that's what we set out to do.

The Need for Speed

In a six-year stretch, 1931 to 1936, Joe Petrali amassed the most national points five times. In 1935, he won every race he entered. He won the National Hill Climb Championship eight straight times (1929 to 1937). In 1937, Petrali set a speed record of 136.183 mph on a 61-cubic-inch V-twin Streamliner at Daytona Beach, Florida.

Because of my experience with snowmobile racing, Vaughn Beals gave me the green light to market the dirt-track team and try to bring back some of the glory that the team had enjoyed in previous decades. All we needed was a marketing plan. I immediately set about getting new uniforms for the spring 1982 racing season. I figured if Harley riders were to win races, they should look good for the cameras.

The first race of the season was on a half-mile track in California. Our lead racer was Jay Springsteen, a former Grand National Champion three years straight (1976–1978). Jay was a natural motorcycle rider. All the other racers idolized him. As a child, he had problems with his hips, and the doctor said to keep him off his feet. So at the age of four or five, his father gave him a scooter, and that became his legs. Jay Springsteen had literally been on bikes almost all his life. He could do amazing things on a motorcycle.

"Dirt-track racers are a completely different breed from, say, Indy drivers. When an Indy driver pulls onto the track, he looks as if he's stifling a yawn; when a dirt-tracker pulls onto the track, he looks as if he's stifling a scream."[7]

—Sam Moses in *Sports Illustrated*, commenting on Jay Springsteen winning the Grand National Championship, 1976

By 1982, Jay had done it all—three Grand National Championships, over two dozen national race titles—and he had been getting national attention, loads of ink in all the major magazines. It somehow affected him psychologically, though; he began to show up at races unable to race. Overcome with apprehension, he would vomit and get dehydrated and sometimes pass out. Once he even had to be taken to the hospital. It didn't happen before every race, but off and on. Psychologists and psychiatrists were consulted, but no one seemed to be able to figure out the problem.

That first race day, I was on the infield of the track when the Harley-Davidson racing truck came rolling in. As it passed, I saw Jay hanging out the back window, vomiting.

Jay Springsteen, Free Spirit

Once after a practice run, Jay pulled a beer from his cooler and began to enjoy some refreshment.

When told that drinking alcohol on the racetrack was a $100 fine, he opened his wallet. "Here's $200," he said. "I'm going to have another one."

At that time, we were spending $700,000 annually to support two racers—Jay Springsteen and another rider from Michigan, Randy Goss. Harley couldn't justify that kind of expenditure on one racer and one part-time racer. For another $150,000, I made the decision to add a third person to the team, a scrawny, baby-faced kid just twenty years old. His name was Scott Parker, and he could fly.

Harley Parts From General Motors

Scott Parker, Randy Goss, and Jay Springsteen were all from Michigan. They had buddies who worked at the major car companies. For years, GM carried specialty parts that only fit on Harley-Davidson motorcycles and could be ordered through the GM dealer.

I required all three riders to cut their hair, sign autographs at local Harley dealerships before races, and wear their uniforms whenever they were at the track. I even had the pockets sewn up on their public-appearance pants so they couldn't put their hands in them during interviews. We also provided them with interview lessons from a professional racetrack announcer who had experience conducting interviews with racers. He videotaped them both before and after the coaching; the differences were vivid.

The public appearance scene was new to them, and they screamed in protest—until the endorsements started coming in. Bell Helmets offered them $25,000 to wear the Bell logo. Leather gloves and boots, oil and gasoline additives followed. I negotiated the contracts, made sure the sponsor's logo was visible in photo shots, and also made sure the boys got paid.

Instead of showing up in jeans, they now looked sharp in their uniforms, conducted themselves professionally in interviews, and began erasing the rowdy carefree image Harley riders (and racers) had enjoyed (or endured) for decades. We created personalities for each racer—wholesome, moral, and polite—that were in stark contrast to those of the rough-edged racers in years past. If the racing team was to be associated with the Harley brand, it was critical that it presented the image we wanted. It had to be an association that conjured up positive thoughts, feelings, and images because the racers were forever to be linked to the Harley brand.

Big Shoes to Fill

One time early in 1982, Scott Parker showed up late for practice on the Springfield, Illinois, dirt-track mile. He rushed into the trailer and madly began to put on his leather uniform. He was a tiny kid, and the suit hung off his scrawny body.

Just as he realized he had the wrong uniform—the name "Springsteen" was clearly visible—the trailer door opened and in walked three-time Grand National Champion Jay Springsteen.

"A little early to try and fill those leathers, isn't it?"

Maybe, but Scott Parker went on to win nine Grand National Championships. He holds the all-time Grand National Dirt Track Championship record of ninety-four race wins (more than twice as many as Jay Springsteen's forty-one) and is a three-time winner of the American Motorcyclist Association Pro Athlete of the Year Award.

The lesson: associate your brand with things—images, expressions, attitudes, qualities, or people—that are positive, and enhance your brand. Use these associations to remind your target market who you are and what you are trying to achieve.

4
BRAND CONSISTENCY

Imagine: You step through the double glass doors into a wonderland, another world entirely. A sense of amazement and adventure emerges from the musky scent of leather with overtones of carnauba wax and something else, something familiar. Machine oil. You fill your lungs, and the smells roll over your tongue.

Beside you is a looking glass, reflecting shades of black and deep orange. Beyond are row upon row of floating raiment, like apparel apparitions—coats and jackets and T-shirts, dozens and dozens of T-shirts. Between the displays and along the walls are lines of gadgets and gewgaws, and the regalia of the open road—boots, rain gear, protective headwear both soft and hard, skullcaps, face masks, and modular helmets with retractable sunshields.

But that's not why you came. The sacrifice and the doing without are at an end. Today is the day.

There is a man there beside you, someone familiar, who smiles at you because he knows what you're thinking. He has felt what you feel. He gently places in your one hand a shiny key, while he grips the other.

You stare at the key and all that it represents. You knew who you were when you woke up this morning, but you feel as if you have been changed since then. Now, at this moment, for the first time in your brief run upon this wonderful planet, you are the owner of a Harley-Davidson motorcycle. You know you can never go back to yesterday. You were a different person then.

Today, you own a Harley. It is a mark in time that you will know and appreciate forever.

This moment is repeated across the globe every day, from Denver to Dubai, Sarasota to Sydney, and all points in between, by hundreds of new riders. Each dealer knows the look, the sense of pride and belonging that go with it. Each dealer is prepared to create that same gratification, to fulfill that dream. Each dealership, wherever it lies on the globe, has certain similar characteristics. Each dealer is an ambassador of the brand.

There is a consistency that begins on Juneau Avenue and extends across the network of Harley-Davidson dealers. Riders have learned what to expect when they cross through the double glass doors. Dealers know what is expected of them, and they know the value of meeting those expectations—consistently.

What Is Brand Consistency?

Harley-Davidson is a multinational corporation; its dealer network spans the globe. If each operated as a separate entity, it would cause confusion among customers, stakeholders, and the general public. Brand consistency unifies the company's highly diverse businesses and geographies, ensures that people recognize and clearly understand what the company offers, and develops credibility and trust over time.

Consistency begins with logo guidelines that work well across all media and all cultures. A specifications book (called a "spec book") contains rules that describe how the logo should appear, its size and shape, colors to be used, typestyles, any taglines, and where the logo should appear on a page or when used in conjunction with other corporate logos and trademarks.

Logos are always used in a similar way on all marketing materials. A single typeface is used, and there are specific guidelines on typography. Specific colors are applied consistently, along similar design styles, so that each marketing piece looks similar to and supports all the other marketing materials. This helps ensure that the brand possesses a unique personality or look, one that enables consumers to distinguish it from competing brands.

For instance, you will never see McDonald's arches in any color but gold (unless rendered in black on white). McDonald's has a three-inch-thick spec book that describes how its logos, trademarks, taglines, and characters can be used. Deviate and suffer swift admonition. Likewise, specific guidelines rule the use of the Bar and Shield. You will never see it in colors other than its familiar orange and black.

Beyond the logos and typefaces, colors and taglines, there is the core message. Brand consistency requires that all parts of the corporate family communicate in a way that supports the core message. For example, if your core message is outstanding quality, a brochure printed on poor-quality paper can undermine your message; if it is superior customer service, a single surly employee can dilute or even destroy all the effort spent to support the core message.

Brand consistency begins a chain of benefits that propel a business toward clarity of purpose and differentiation in the market. The consistent application of logos and messages and promises leads to recognition and familiarity, which leads to trust and confidence. That consistency is further evidenced in the organization's employees and how they present the brand.

The more consistent the public's experience with your brand, the more people trust that the brand will live up to their expectations. It's a long-term proposition. Leading brands become leading brands because they have had many years of brand consistency.

Dealer Development

Part of the job was to visit dealerships throughout the country. It served as a good way to get to know our dealer network and understand their customers' needs. As a bonus, I got to meet (and often ride with) some great people.

Vaughn Beals, Harley-Davidson's president, and I were on our way back to Milwaukee from New England. Along the way, we visited a few Harley dealers. One Saturday, we pulled into a small parking lot with a tattered sign: Harley-Davidson Motorcycles. The dealership was little more than an old shed. It had a dirt floor and a single light bulb that hung from its exposed ceiling. In a corner, a 50-gallon barrel was filled with empty beer cans. We waited an hour to see the owner, but he never came in. He was probably off riding somewhere. It left an indelible impression.

> "Problems are in the office. Solutions are in the field."
>
> —Harley proverb

It wasn't the only dealership like that, either. Some were run-down, located in rough neighborhoods, or presented a dirty and unkempt impression. This only served to perpetuate the rowdy, wicked biker image portrayed in movies—not the kind of places Mom and Dad would want to bring the kids on a Saturday afternoon.

Japanese bike stores were run by businessmen, guys out to make a return on investment. Their showrooms were new, their service areas clean and orderly. Many Harley dealerships were run by enthusiasts, riders who wanted to buy their own motorcycles at dealer cost and spend their time riding.

These dealership visits also unearthed another problem. On a sunny September day in Albuquerque, I was having a cup of coffee with the local Harley dealer when his telephone rang. It was his banker, and he took the call.

They chatted for a little while, and then the dealer said, "Joe, I want you to put me on credit hold until next March. That's right. I've got fifteen motorcycles in stock, and I can sell these same motorcycles four or five times before then. I'll call you in March. You can take me off of the credit hold list, and I'll take delivery of all the bikes I have on order from the factory and deliver them to my customers."

After he hung up, I asked him why he had requested to be put on credit hold. This was a highly successful dealership; he sold 150 motorcycles per year.

"Well," he said, "nobody rides till spring, so nobody wants his bike until spring. Why should I let those bikes sit on my floor and pay interest on them? In March, I'll call Joe and tell him to release the money. I can deliver a hundred bikes or more by the end of April."

He had a point. But Harley had over six hundred dealers, and many of them did the very same thing. Most customers don't want to take delivery of their new bikes until riding weather, so why should the dealer stock them until then? The dealer preferred to let the bikes sit all winter in York. That way, the factory picked up all the interest and storage costs.

I pointed out to the dealer how this created a cash-flow nightmare on Juneau Avenue and had a negative effect on quality.

"Look," he said. "I know how to run my business. That's my job. As for the rest of it, that's your problem."

And he was right. It was.

These are just two examples of the problems faced by Harley-Davidson in the early 1980s. Our dealer network was a mishmash of engine mechanics and riding enthusiasts who had varying ideas about how to run a Harley dealership. In short, there was no consistency from dealer to dealer, and that couldn't help but reflect poorly on the Harley brand.

At that time, about 1,000 dealers sold about 30,000 motorcycles a year. Today, 1,400 dealers sell over 300,000 annually at dealerships around the world. That means every dealer is selling almost seven times as many bikes today as he sold thirty years ago.

There are three principal reasons for this sales growth at the dealerships. All three helped bring consistency to the Harley-Davidson dealer network. First was the Strategic Growth Plan, a detailed five-year business plan that Harley insisted every dealer provide and follow. The second was the Designer Store Program, a complete remodel of virtually every Harley dealership throughout the world. The last was called

Bonus Bucks. This program came about as a direct result of my visit to the Albuquerque dealership. It was controversial, and it was crucial to our survival.

Strategic Growth Plan

At the annual dealer meeting in 1983, Vaughn Beals laid down the law. After thanking the dealers for their loyalty through the lean years, Beals chastised them for their attitude toward owners of Japanese bikes, and he berated them for the lackadaisical manner in which they ran their dealerships. He insisted that all dealers would meet the Harley standards for atmosphere, stocking procedures, product demonstration, and promotion.

"We will first try to do it by persuasion and training, by making sure that you fully understand our common goals and direction," said Beals. "But rest assured we will do it. Our future and yours make it mandatory."

Beals then presented the company's long-term growth plan, a plan that called for a 15 percent annual growth rate, a doubling of sales in just five years (1983 to 1988). It was interesting to watch the dealer reactions. A lot of heads were shaking. Double sales in five years? Many dealers didn't believe it was possible. Others believed it could be done, but they felt they might be too old or too set in their ways to go along for the ride.

Management required each dealer to draw up a Strategic Growth Plan. Each plan included an operations plan, financial plan, human resources plan, and marketing plan. How will you double your sales over the next five years? How will you plan for it? How will you finance it? What new employees will you need to hire and train? If the dealer didn't have a plan or didn't know how to create one, Harley provided it for him.

Meanwhile, our supply chain had to be prepared, too. Management visited all the vendors to tell them of Harley's plans to double capacity. Just as we did with the dealers, we asked the vendors how they would prepare for it. About 25 percent said no to expansion, and they had to be replaced.

Designer Store Program

Many dealerships did not live up to minimum appearance standards. To be blunt, some were just dumps. One dealership in Wyoming had a dirt floor. Others were tiny places with little room to move when there were motorcycles in the showroom. Still others were large warehouses with lofty ceilings and concrete floors.

> "If the showroom looks like a warehouse, customers expect warehouse pricing."
>
> —Harley proverb

In 1986, we launched the Designer Store Program, which encouraged dealers to consider the selling atmosphere they were presenting to their customers. If it did not meet minimum Harley standards, the dealer was asked to remodel or build a new store entirely.

A California design firm was hired to develop standardized requirements for the dealerships. Exterior and interior designs were to be included. These were not to be cookie-cutter stores. Each would be unique but with similar characteristics in terms of square footage, showroom floor area, service areas, and private offices. From the outside, no dealership would look the same as any other dealership. Exteriors would look indigenous to the area. For instance, the Mesa, Arizona, dealership was remodeled to resemble a pueblo. The Des Moines, Iowa, store looked like a big barn (complete with "hogs" inside).

On the inside, each dealership needed to have only one of each new model on the sales floor. The bikes were to be elevated, spotlighted for drama, and surrounded with colorful displays of MotorClothes and Motor Accessories. Later, the rules became even more detailed, specifying the types of display racks that could be used, the paint colors and color of carpet that could be used, and so on. The objective was to maximize sales per square foot.

Bell Cow Theory

In Wisconsin, dairy farmers pick their best cow and hang a bell around its neck. All the other cows follow its lead.

Harley always chooses its best dealers to roll out a new program. If those dealers are successful, the rest will follow.

Many dealers could not (or would not) risk the cost of a remodel. Following our bell cow theory, Harley picked one of its leading dealers to remodel his dealership—a complete exterior makeover, new interior colors, lighting, displays, the works. Harley-Davidson even loaned the dealer the money on a five-year note.

He paid it back in eighteen months.

That did it. Other dealers quickly signed up for the program.

> "All Harley riders are part of a greater family, but their local store is their next of kin."
>
> —Kirk Topel, Harley-Davidson dealer

Today, each dealership strives to have its own personality. Riders tend to think of their local dealership as "their" store. When traveling, they visit other stores—buy a souvenir, learn about the surrounding area and the best places to ride—partly to measure them against their own dealership back home.

Despite their individuality, all dealerships share common traits that were established by the Designer Store Program. All contribute to Harley-Davidson's brand consistency.

Bonus Bucks

Another way Harley sought to build and maintain brand consistency among its dealers was through a program called Bonus Bucks, launched in 1983.

The Bonus Bucks program was modeled after similar programs in the automobile industry. Auto manufacturers had been using incentive programs for years in an effort to efficiently plan their production and cash-flow requirements. Why couldn't Harley do the same? I simply modified the auto industry's program to solve specific problems associated with the motorcycle industry and Harley's unique circumstances.

Bonus Bucks was probably the most controversial program ever instituted at Harley-Davidson. However, it was crucial to Harley's success. Cash-flow problems caused by dealers like the one in Albuquerque and inconsistencies in the presentation of the Harley brand throughout the dealer network had to be resolved. Ultimately, Harley either implemented the Bonus Bucks program or faced bankruptcy.

Here's how it worked. Dealer margins were immediately changed from 25 percent to 20 percent on all big V-twins. A dealer could *earn* that 5 percent margin back if he would:

1. Continue to take shipment of new bikes throughout the year

2. Hold an open house each fall (when new models came in)

3. Use co-op advertising

4. Offer demonstration rides

5. Participate in the sample program

6. Provide service training to all his mechanics

The continuous shipment of bikes throughout the year was essential. Without this policy, the company's cash flow would have been a mess, and Harley would not have survived. Seasonal manufacturing would have created a terrible problem for quality control because continuous manufacturing is essential to ensure consistent quality.

> "When you run a McDonald's franchise, you do it McDonald's way. If you don't like arches, you don't run a McDonald's. To get national identity, you have to give up some freedom."
>
> —Vaughn Beals, 1983 dealer meeting

The open house was a promotional event that served to introduce the new bikes. Though it was not crucial, dealers understood the benefits, and most of them readily agreed to this portion of the program.

Co-op advertising helped the company control the message used throughout the dealer network, but it limited dealers in their ability to appeal directly to their local communities. They had limited advertising budgets, and many dealers wanted to spend their money on local advertising and promotions, rather than simply tagging a corporate ad. Over time, we modified this portion of the program and allowed more flexibility for dealers to do localized advertising. But all ads had to be approved by corporate.

The requirement that all dealers offer demonstration rides also met stiff resistance. Some dealers would not even let potential customers sit on the bikes for fear they might scratch the gas tank. Who would buy a bike if they couldn't ride it first? Or even sit on it?

Harley needed a minimum number of commitments from dealers in order to get quantity pricing on accessories. The sample program was a way to expose these new products to end users. Harley sold packages of sample accessories to dealers. A big box would arrive at the dealership, along with an invoice. Inside the box might be half a dozen accessory products, things like exhaust pipes, air intakes, and mirrors. Since most riders love to trick out their bikes, management thought that these items would sell if dealers would only stock them. To minimize dealers' risk, Harley allowed the items to be returned for full credit if they hadn't sold in six months, provided the packaging was undamaged. (As a form of protest, some dealers simply stowed the box, unopened, in a back room for six months and then sent it back for full credit.) Most of the items sold well. A few didn't and were returned.

Service training was not readily accepted. Many dealers' service personnel were natural gearheads anyway. Now the dealer would be required to send his people to service training school and certify each mechanic. The purpose was to build trust in their reliability among Harley customers. But as quality improved on the bikes, the credibility associated with training certification became less necessary. This requirement became more flexible over time.

The most controversial part of all, of course, was how Harley financed the program. Harley management felt that one way to get the dealer network to implement the company's long-term growth plan was to appeal to their pocketbooks: "We'll give you Bonus Bucks, up to 5 percent, if you follow the plan." That was the incentive.

When the Bonus Bucks program was announced, dealers were in favor of it, at first. "Bonus" sounded like a good thing. On the surface, it appeared they could receive an additional 5 percent margin on every motorcycle they sold over a certain number.

But how would Harley pay for the program? Simple. The company took 5 percent profit off the dealer wholesale price. Typically, dealers received a 25 percent margin on bike sales. It had been that way for decades. Margins immediately went from 25 percent to 20 percent on all sales of big V-twins. A dealer could earn back the 5 percent difference in Bonus Bucks if he adhered to all the rules set forth in the program.

Management's theory was that, through his participation, a dealer could enhance his sales skills, develop his technicians' skills, and benefit from the corporate advertising program. By doing so, he would earn the same margin as before (20 percent plus 5 percent Bonus Bucks) while improving his operation and creating more sales to add to his profit. That was the theory. That was the Bonus Bucks program.

Dealers hated it.

The 25 percent margin they had always received was being taken away from them. Many were ready to revolt. Some flat out refused to go along. A few threatened to desert Harley and sell Japanese bikes instead. The Bonus Bucks program nearly tore the dealer network apart. Thirty-two dealers broke away from the company's Dealer's Advisory Council to form their own dissident group, the National Harley-Davidson Dealers Alliance, whose stated purpose was to challenge the questionable decisions made by management.

Vaughn Beals would not back down. He was determined to create brand consistency among all the dealerships. "Sooner or later, it will mean that those dealers who can't or won't meet the standards will have to make some new career plans," said Beals.

The alliance persisted. Many complained that Harley management had simply cut margins to line their own pockets. In an unprecedented move for a nonpublic company, Harley opened its books to senior officers of the Dealers Alliance. Numbers don't lie. The financial statements assured the dealers that no one at headquarters was getting rich off the reduced margins. It also revealed just how precarious the situation really was.

This calmed the storm temporarily, but it took several years and a great deal of bargaining with dissident dealers before the tempest eventually subsided—not because either side ever agreed with the other. There are dealers to this day who feel Vaughn Beals was too overbearing, and his attitude of "my way or the highway" still rankles many. But eventually sales and profits climbed dramatically, and the company began to prosper to the point that the arguments became less heated and more infrequent. Soon, the dissident dealers were complaining less about margins and more about not having enough bikes to sell.

Bonus Bucks ensured cash flow for the company, a consistent manufacturing production build to ensure quality, and brand consistency throughout the dealer network. It was at the crux of Harley-Davidson's recovery and ultimate success.

Harley-Davidson University

Dealers of Japanese bikes tended to be businessmen first, riders second (if at all). Most Harley dealers were (and are) enthusiasts first. We needed to show Harley dealers how to be businessmen. So we resurrected Harley-Davidson University in 1983 to teach them.

HDU (as it is commonly known) was first established in 1917. At that time, a majority of motorcycle production was devoted to the war effort. Harley recognized the need for military quartermasters and mechanics to know the motorcycles inside and out. The first students were nine corporals from Fort Sam Houston, Texas, who took a three-week intensive course. After World War I, the school was opened to any mechanic at any authorized dealer.

The service school had always been primarily just that—a service school that taught the mechanics of motorcycles. Our dealers knew the mechanics of motorcycles; they needed to learn the mechanics of business. So Harley hired outside experts—non-Harley-Davidson employees—as professors of marketing, finance, accounting, and merchandising. These learned academics taught dealers and their employees how to create profitable businesses that sold more motorcycles, merchandise, and mechanical services, and helped establish and operate add-on profit centers like motorcycle insurance and bike financing programs.

School started in January, before the big V-Twin Expo in early February. The timing was intentional. The V-Twin Expo featured aftermarket products. The expo was not allowed to use the Harley-Davidson name because most of the aftermarket parts were not sanctioned by Harley. Nevertheless, many Harley dealers traditionally attended the expo, where they often purchased aftermarket products that could be resold to their customers.

Harley-Davidson University created confidence and enthusiasm among the dealers. You could see it in their faces. They were learning things they had never learned before, things they knew they would need to grow their businesses, such as financing and leasing arrangements, merchandising, and how to prepare for the spring selling season.

The university environment also offered Harley-Davidson an opportunity to display all the new Motor Accessories, aftermarket products that were supplied by the company, a whole month before the V-Twin Expo. The dealers spent their money on genuine Harley-Davidson aftermarket products *before* they went to the expo.

Today, Harley-Davidson University trains dealers, technicians, employees, and others in just about every conceivable subject related to Harley-Davidson motorcycles. Classes include retail sales techniques, merchandising, promotion, customer service, financing, insurance, operations, and human resources.

Harley-Davidson University helps establish brand consistency by ensuring the maintenance of all Harley-Davidson motorcycles in a consistent manner, by creating guidelines for operations, and by instilling a sense of empowerment among all the dealers. They are trained to be the masters of their fate, the captains of their (dealer)ships—but each is trained in the Harley way.

The Double-Humped Camel

The motorcycle sales cycle was established years before my tenure in the business. Much like the car business, next year's models were introduced in the fall of the prior year. Our factories in Milwaukee and York manufactured to this schedule and had been doing so for decades.

All the new models were introduced to the dealers at Harley's annual dealer meeting held every September. Typically meetings opened with a pep talk, a state of the company address, a sales presentation, and the unveiling of new models. Then district managers would meet with individual dealers to take orders. This annual dealer meeting was supposed to be Harley's first opportunity to show off the new bikes and take orders. But it wasn't.

Many riders and some of the dealers attended the annual rally in Sturgis each August, where Harley had all the new model bikes on display. So by September, some of the dealers had already seen them—but worse, so had many customers who were at Sturgis. As a group, the dealers rightly felt they should be the first ones to know about the new bikes. They resented it when some of their customers returned from the rally and told them what was new. In terms of introducing the new bikes, the September meeting became just a formality, a chance to press the flesh and write up orders.

September was also when Harley took orders for MotorClothes. Dealers placed their holiday orders in September for delivery in October. November and December were typically the best sales periods for MotorClothes.

Dealers were getting big sales bumps of both new model bikes and MotorClothes late in the year. Their annual sales chart looked something like figure 4.1.

In this sales scenario, stocking inventory and turnover became a problem in Milwaukee. We had to warehouse and build inventory all summer long for shipment after the September sales meeting and then wait for the reorders in October or November, after the dealers had a chance to move the products we shipped to them after the meeting.

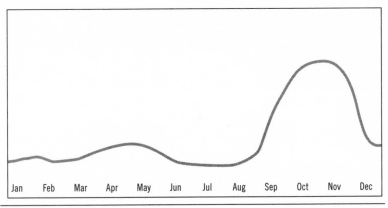

| Jan | Feb | Mar | Apr | May | Jun | Jul | Aug | Sep | Oct | Nov | Dec |

Figure 4.1: The single-humped camel.

"Adjust your selling cycle to suit your customers, not the factory."

—Harley proverb

In a bold strategic move in the early 1990s, I convinced the marketing team to hold the dealer meeting in July, before the big rally in Sturgis. This offered a number of advantages. First, hotel rooms in Las Vegas were cheaper in July, so money was saved there. Next, Harley could show off next year's model bikes before anyone, dealers or customers, saw them in Sturgis. Dealers could then place their orders for motorcycles in July and take delivery in August. As an added bonus, our retail customers had the opportunity to see and test ride the new bikes at Sturgis.

That first year, Harley had to adjust the timing of the entire product development process. Design, prototype development, testing, brochures, service manuals, purchasing, ending inventory—everything had to be changed and moved forward by several months to coordinate with the new delivery and selling season.

Dealers placed initial orders for MotorClothes and Motor Accessories at July's annual dealer meeting—not enough for the big holiday season, but a sufficient amount to stock their stores with the latest product. In this way, dealers were able to see what was selling before placing orders for the holiday selling season. They placed their stocking orders in late September and October for delivery by the holidays; they knew exactly what to order and how much.

Now dealers had two big selling opportunities: in August, when all their new-model bikes arrived, and at the holidays, when holiday shoppers stocked up on MotorClothes. Dealers' new sales curve looked like a double-humped camel, figure 4.2.

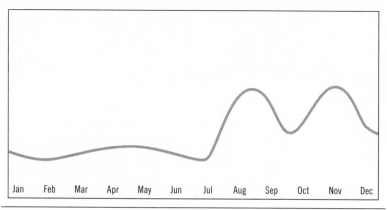

Figure 4.2: The double-humped camel.

The double-humped camel increased the turnover of inventory and cash flow. It gave dealers two selling seasons. It also created excitement for the new motorcycles among customers months before the Japanese introduced their new bikes each year. This was another left turn while the industry was turning right.

Stretching the Advertising Budget

To compete with lightweight European imports, Harley-Davidson began producing lightweight motorcycles in 1948 with the introduction of the model 125cc S in Milwaukee. Later, when Japanese imports increased, the competition in the lightweight market became even steeper. Harley improved its core competency in the design and production of smaller motorcycles (and increased production capacity) when it acquired a minority interest in the Aermacchi Motorcycle Company of Verona, Italy, in 1960.

The Italian company had expertise in small four- and two-stroke engines as well as lightweight entry-level motorcycles. For the next several years, Harley marketed a combination of US- and Italian-built small bikes, until 1967, when all production and engineering were shifted to Italy. Harley acquired full control of Aermacchi's motorcycle production.

Unfortunately, Harley dealers couldn't sell the lightweight bikes. The Harley-Davidson lineup didn't compete well against the simpler, faster, more reliable, and less expensive Japanese bikes that were beginning to flood the market. In the mid-1970s, Harley-Davidson decided to get out of the lightweight motorcycle business and sold the company in 1977.

After the sale of the company, Harley ended up with 3,000 Aermacchi motorcycles sitting in a Milwaukee warehouse with no place to go. We couldn't get rid of them. Both the dealer network and the retail customer had seen enough of these small imitation Harleys. What do you do with 3,000 motorcycles that no one wants?

The marketing department struck a deal with a company that specialized in exchanging distressed merchandise for advertising time on TV and radio. In exchange for the 3,000 motorcycles, Harley received $300,000 in TV advertising, or $100 a bike.

A TV commercial was produced for about $25,000. The ad featured just-retired football star Dick Butkus. A three-man agency from Chicago that specialized in running low-budget TV spots for home appliance product blowouts created a hard-sell message that invited customers to come in and test the 40-plus miles per gallon mileage of a Harley-Davidson motorcycle. Called a "tag spot," the TV commercial lasted twenty-six seconds, with the remaining four seconds to be filled by three dealer tags. Each tag would feature a picture of the dealer principal along with the name and location of his dealership.

Harley launched the program in the New York / New Jersey metro area, the country's largest TV market. At a meeting with the local dealers, we proposed the co-op television advertising program: Harley would pay up front for the media costs, then bill the dealer for his share of the ads. Dealers could be featured in one or more ads, but all the dealers had to participate or the program would be scrapped.

The co-op rate was fifty-fifty—Harley paid for half of the program, and the other half was split among the fifteen local dealers. All of the dealers chose to participate. Harley bartered the lightweight motorcycles for $300,000 in media and billed half the value of the advertising to the dealers. Each of the fifteen dealers paid $10,000.

We then took the $150,000 received from the New York / New Jersey dealers and went to Buffalo, New York, a B-sized market with less expensive media costs. It was the same basic plan. We bought the TV media and billed half the cost, or $75,000, to the Buffalo-area dealers. Then we took their $75,000 and moved to smaller markets and repeated the same process.

After the Buffalo and New York / New Jersey trials, the co-op advertising proved to be so successful, we added several hundred thousand dollars to the program and rolled it out on a nationwide basis. We started with large markets, billed the area dealers for half the cost, and took those monies to a smaller market. All dealers in a market had to participate, and we required a minimum media buy of 100 gross rating points (GRPs). (This is an advertising term that means we needed to reach at least 100 percent of our market one time, or 50 percent of our market two times, or 20 percent of our market five times, and so on.)

The program was a huge success. What began as a problem of unloading 3,000 unwanted lightweight motorcycles turned into a nationwide dealer co-op TV advertising campaign worth over $2,000,000—a small amount in today's dollars, but a lot for the times. Dealers received huge visibility in their markets for a fraction of the cost they would have likely paid on their own. And Harley managed to build a consistent advertising image for its dealer network.

Another win-win.

5
BRAND WELFARE

Imagine: In front of you are two Sportsters, one an XL 1200, the other an 883 Hugger. They carve the air to each side as you slide into their slipstream. In your mirrors, you see the line of motorcycles narrowing to the horizon, a white dashed line retreating between bright reflections of chrome.

To your right is a 1340 Wide Glide with forward controls and a bobbed rear fender, its engine rumbling in rhythm with your own. Its rider, covered head to boot in black, sits stiffly, long arms aped over the custom handlebars. The black helmet slowly turns to you, one arm rises, and a gloved fist punches the air. You raise your fist in response.

A signpost reads, "Delafield 6, Milwaukee 28." At an overpass, a family dressed in bright blues and yellows waves as you pass beneath; the little boy, not more than seven, holds a tiny American flag. More flags await you at the next overpass.

The journey has come to an end, the ride complete. Pride swells within you, and you raise your hand once more—to the flags, to the families, to the ride, and to Jerry's Kids.

Your boots touch down as you roll to a stop. You remove your helmet, and the cool slaps you aware—aware of the steaming iron and the gleaming chrome, aware of the music, and of the crowd. The Wide Glide rolls in beside you, and the rider sets the bike and dismounts. There is a moment of anticipation before the buckle is unsnapped and gloved hands raise the helmet high in the air.

The crowd erupts. This is Harley heaven, and its namesake has come home. Mr. Honda cannot ride his motorcycle from Los Angeles to Milwaukee and raise $100,000 for a worthy cause. Willie G. Davidson can.

With him are you and 40,000 others who have come to help aid in a cause that Harley employees, dealers, and riders have supported since 1980. From Houston, Seattle, Boston, and Biloxi, you have pledged to raise money for the Muscular Dystrophy Association (MDA) to fund research and programs for both adults and children with this crippling disease.

Harley-Davidson knows it is the right thing to do, and not just because the kids are so deserving. Certainly, there's that. But it's also good business. Research has shown time and again that people prefer to do business with good corporate citizens, those companies that benefit their communities in a positive manner, as well as those companies that look out for their customers.

What Is Brand Welfare?

It is not enough to simply build a brand. That branded image must be nurtured and reinforced. Brand welfare is the maintenance, over time, of the brand's desired image. By aligning the brand with a cause favored by customers, you ensure the future welfare of the brand.

A Commitment to Your Community

When Abraham Maslow developed his hierarchy of needs, he placed the desire to leave a legacy at the top of the pyramid.[8] *Self-actualization* is man's desire to achieve his full potential (or as the US Army advertises, "Be all you can be"). Donating to a cause allows us to reach for that greater moral high ground, to achieve our personal self-actualization.

Some donate to a charity because of a personal attachment. If a loved one has diabetes, supporting the American Diabetes Association may seem like an ideal way to show your devotion while helping to find a cure. A pharmaceutical company heavily invested in cancer research might support the American Cancer Society.

It isn't shameful to list tax breaks among the reasons for giving. This country's well-being relies on public donations. The government encourages contributions to good causes by providing taxpayers with deductions for making those contributions. Tax savings related to charitable giving can be substantial, both during one's lifetime and through estate giving. These incentives do make it easier to be generous.

But the tax benefits are seldom cited as the main reason for a person's charitable contributions. There is something else we receive in return. Helping others rejuvenates us in ways that another vacation, a fatter portfolio, or more stuff just cannot do. Maslow said so. We all want to feel useful, to find meaning in our lives. Serving others can help us find our true calling, improve our mental health, and boost our overall sense of joy.

Reasons for Giving

According to the Center on Philanthropy at Indiana University, people give to charities for a variety of reasons, including:

- To gain a feeling of satisfaction and value from helping others or saving lives
- To leave a lasting positive imprint on the community

- To promote or perpetuate a certain philosophy or belief
- To memorialize a friend or loved one
- To give back to the community from which one has earned one's wealth
- To be a leader in one's community
- To gain tax benefits

Volunteerism and charitable contributions are good business, too. Beyond the tax deduction, there are solid financial reasons to give back to your community. For one, it can raise your business profile and bring in more customers or clients.

Many businesses sponsor charitable events. Others include their charitable work in their advertising, adding copy such as "50 percent of all profits will be donated to [name of charity]." People like being able to combine their pleasure in patronizing a business with the pleasure of helping others. Those companies that donate to a cause, one that their customers can support, will enhance their image and build loyalty to the brand.

Giving is contagious. The more you give, the more you want to give. And the more visible your gift, the more others are encouraged to give. While you may feel that giving as an individual has no lasting effect—what can just one person do?—you likely recognize the power of your gift when combined with the gifts of others. You become part of a larger group, a community whose collective goals are defined by the organization receiving the gift.

Giving is good for the soul, but it's good for your bottom line, too.

Community Involvement

How should you choose which charity to support? There are so many, and most are so worthy.

"There is no better exercise for your heart than reaching down and helping to lift someone up."

—Bernard Meltzer

Each individual, company, or government has reasons for supporting a country, cause, or organization. Governments have their political reasons. Individuals have their pet causes and legacies and tax benefits. Corporations are different. Their choice of giving cannot be solely influenced by politics or legacies or causes or needs. While corporations may provide substantial contributions to charities, especially if they use their brand weight to encourage individuals to support those same charities, companies, particularly public companies, have a financial obligation to their owners to maximize the value of any charitable contribution through both financial incentives and goodwill to be gained. A company's choice of charity should support its cause, its community, and its bottom line in equal measure.

For a company, the first step in choosing a charity is to define its community. This may not only be the geographic area—city, county, state, or region—in which it resides or operates. It could also be the industry—suppliers, distribution channels, customers, and prospects.

Once defined, the next step is to invest in that community. These are the people who help support your business. What better way is there to honor that relationship than to give back? Moreover, some believe that successful members of a community have a moral responsibility to help those in the community who are less fortunate. The greater the success, the greater the responsibility.

Small business or large, there are many benefits to community involvement:

- You enhance your image in the community.
- You achieve greater visibility for your company.
- You enlarge your network of business contacts.
- You can make a significant impact on your bottom line.

Choose the organization that best fits your company profile. Then work with them (and make them work with you, too).

Let's take a look at three examples of giving that will help you while you help others:

1. Donate a percentage of the sales.
2. Ask key vendors for contributions.
3. Sponsor a scholarship.

You could donate a percentage of your sales during a one-day-a-year event or a whole month (or, like Newman's Own and a few other companies, on an ongoing basis). Promote it as "We Care Day" or "[name of the charity] Month." Ask the charity to do a mailing to its list of contributors and friends inviting them to do business with you. Include a coupon or certificate for a discount in the mailing.

If the charity has access to a celebrity, ask if they can arrange an appearance at your next function as a part of the fundraising program. Set up an autograph table or have a photographer take pictures in exchange for a donation. For example, Harley-Davidson used Playboy Bunnies to help raise money for the MDA.

Once a year, send a handwritten note to several of your key customers thanking them for their support. In the note, tell them that, in appreciation, you are making a cash contribution in their name to a charitable organization. Ask the customer to match your contribution. Publicize the partner giving, and receive the appreciation of your customers while the charity receives your combined support.

Scholarships at the high school or college level make good sense. For example, a company provides a $1,000 scholarship each year to a deserving student in a specific department at a local college. In addition, the student is offered an internship at the company. The school chooses the recipient from among several worthy candidates.

A scholarship program provides the student with much-needed funds while your company gets recognition at a prestigious school and a top-notch employee. The visibility and good-guy image help when it comes time to recruit employees.

Community involvement enhances your image, creates name recognition, and enlarges your network of contacts. Besides, it's a great way to meet some nice people.

The Harley community is a vast community that bespeaks the universal appeal of the Harley brand. To many motorcycle enthusiasts, Harley-Davidson is family. Giving as a family helps bring together family members for a common purpose. Service work automatically connects you with an infectious, can-do community of kindred volunteers.

The Muscular Dystrophy Association

A charity can provide value to employees and customers beyond the dollars they raise. Companies generally look for philanthropic partners who understand and work with a company's brand strategy. There is also the intrinsic feeling of goodness that comes from helping others.

We knew that Harley-Davidson needed to change its image. By supporting a popular charitable organization, one that families—mom, dad, and the kids—could support, we felt that we could broaden Harley's audience. We needed to partner with a charity that would help sweep away the bad-guy image that had dogged the brand for too long. The company established a list of criteria:

- The organization had to have universal appeal—all ages, races, genders, and income levels.

- The organization had to give a high percentage of its funds raised to research and rehabilitation rather than fundraising and administrative expenses.

- The organization had to have a nationwide network of offices that could tie in with the Harley dealership network.

- The organization had to have significant public visibility and a favorable reputation among all population sectors.

The MDA offered all that and more. Its universal appeal—who doesn't like kids?—had enormous traction among all population segments; it claimed the second-highest percentage of contributions to research among all major charities; it had local offices in every major city in the country; and since 1965, Jerry Lewis had hosted the Labor Day Telethon, raising awareness of the cause and raising millions in the process. The MDA was a perfect fit for Harley-Davidson. Such a worthy cause brought together the Harley community like no other opportunity could.

MDA was created in 1950 by a group of adults with muscular dystrophy, parents of children with muscular dystrophy, and a physician-scientist studying the disorder. The nonprofit health agency is dedicated to curing muscular dystrophy, amyotrophic lateral sclerosis (ALS, also known as Lou Gehrig's disease), and related ailments. The association provides funding for research, support services, advocacy, and education. MDA has more than 200 offices across the United States and supports more than 330 research projects around the world.

"I Gave at the Office!"

According to the Center on Philanthropy at Indiana University, when employees are asked to make a donation at their place of work:

- Over two-thirds want to know the impact of their donations.
- They want the information shared to be both personally moving and quantifiably compelling.
- Successful campaigns find ways to communicate how gifts translate into progress and social change.

The Harley community has responded admirably—to the tune of about $80 million at this writing. An understanding of the impact their gifts make helps inspire giving. MDA distributes fundraising information liberally. The impact of its efforts is shared with employees, dealers, and customers throughout the Harley community.

The partnership has proven helpful to Harley, too. For instance, in the 1980s, Harley-Davidson's market share in California was half what it was in the rest of the United States. In California, bikers rode Japanese bikes. Harley had a good dealer network but was being outspent in the media by Honda and Kawasaki. We saw another turn-left opportunity—our competition owned TV, so we would find another way to reach our customers. Harley opted to hold a dealer event in the biggest market in California, Los Angeles.

First, we picked a date when motorcycle enthusiasts would be in town. A motocross race was scheduled at the LA Coliseum, and we strategically booked the Staples Center across the street and hosted a motorcycle show. We called it "Artistry in Iron," and almost every California dealer was there, bringing custom and antique motorcycles to the show. We put over 350 bikes on display and invited vendors to rent a booth to help defray costs.

We needed to line up a charity, an organization that could spread the word (we didn't have money for TV, radio, or much else). One of the first charities we spoke to was the MDA. They saw the opportunity to raise money and awareness among attendees; we saw the opportunity to create interest and publicity for the event through their network.

Next, I called the manager of the Doobie Brothers to ask if the band would be willing to help us out and attend. It was for a good cause, and the answer was yes.

Good for Your Health, Too

According to research from the University of California, Los Angeles, those who participate in charitable fundraising are generally healthier and live longer.

Lastly, we hired Playboy Bunnies to help create excitement. At their booth, a sign read, "Have your photo taken with a Playboy Bunny for a donation to MDA." Riders lined up ten deep for the cause (OK, maybe for the Bunnies).

Harley had a built-in audience across the street—motocross and motorcycle riders. The association sponsoring their race welcomed the added attraction of Harley-Davidson next door and mentioned our event in their advertising and promotions. MDA publicized the event through their publicity channels. Playboy publicized it. And the California dealer network publicized it.

Thousands attended. MDA raised money for research and support services. Motocross loved the added benefit for their fans. Harley dealers got invaluable visibility. And the Bunnies had fun, too.

Another win-win.

The Rallies: Laconia

In addition to its backing of MDA, Harley takes a more direct approach to supporting its community.

Picturesque Laconia, near Lake Winnipesaukee in rural New Hampshire, hosts one of the country's largest rallies beginning on the Saturday of the weekend before each Father's Day and ending on Father's Day. Known as Laconia Motorcycle Week, the rally draws attendees from all over the world, swelling this sleepy community of 14,000 to over 375,000 during the nine-day event.

Most often referred to as "Laconia," the Loudon Classic motorcycle race, held in nearby Loudon, New Hampshire, is the longest-running motorcycle race in the country. The rally's origins date back to 1916, when a few hundred bikers first gathered along Weirs Beach. The first

motorcycle race began there in 1923, and the hill-climb competition followed soon after.

During the 1960s, Laconia experienced the kind of trouble too often
associated with bikers at that time. In 1965, violence broke out between
the police and gangs of motorcycle riders, most of whom rode Harleys.
Police and city officials decided to limit the rally to a three-day weekend,
and this brought about a decline in the number of participants.

The Weirs Beach Riot

A week before the Laconia rally in 1965, two New Hampshire state
laws were enacted. One allowed police to arrest riders loitering in
groups of three or more; the other provided for fines and impris-
onment for anyone causing property damage. This only served to
aggravate the thousands of bikers who flocked to Laconia each year.

On June 19, 2,000 motorcycle fans threw rocks, burned cars, and
damaged buildings during a night of rioting. Laconia police and state
troopers, wearing steel riot helmets and gas masks, arrested more
than 100. Most rode Harleys.

Not until the early 1990s, when Laconia businesses joined with local
Harley motorcycle groups to found the Laconia Motorcycle Rally and
Race Week Association, did the race return to its original nine days.
Today, the association organizes and schedules all events, issues vendor
licenses, and promotes the rally nationwide.

Harley-Davidson has been a major supporter of Laconia. The primary
purposes of the rally have always been to provide a good time for riders
and to promote the sport that brings them so much pleasure. Harley has
lived that message at Laconia since its inception.

The Rallies: Daytona

What began as a beach race in 1937 has evolved into the Daytona 200, a
68-lap 200-mile motorcycle race held at Daytona International Speedway
in Daytona Beach, Florida, the first full week of March. The original race
course ran north along the beach for a mile and a half, through a banked
turn, and then onto the paved roadway for the trip south. Start times for
these early races were dictated by the local tide tables.

The race is not the only attraction. Hard sand and warm weather
are perfect excuses to have a beach party, and Daytona soon became a

popular gathering place for motorcycle enthusiasts. Riders from all over the world—as many as 450,000—gather there each March to show off their bikes. Some of them bring the bikes they have been working on all winter, modifying them into what some refer to as motorcycle works of art. Others customize their bikes with a variety of Harley parts and accessories. Each owner tries to outdo the next. It's called the Ride-In Show, and it attracts some unusual artistry in iron. Many bikers spend all winter customizing their motorcycles, and Daytona is the first opportunity to show off their work. While they compete for cash and trophies, riders and fans get a close-up view of these rolling sculptures.

Just as at Laconia, Daytona Bike Week was not always a peaceful celebration of motorcycle mania. Races on the beach were organized, but the events surrounding the race were not.

Occasionally, the early March race date would coincide with colleges' spring breaks. The flood of visitors from these two different communities overburdened the local populace and caused law enforcement officers and city officials to fear the bikers (apparently, the college students were less frightening). As conflicts escalated between these disparate groups, relations between the bikers and law enforcement officials continued to worsen.

In 1986, a special task force was convened at Harley-Davidson's request. We met with the local chamber of commerce and city police in an effort to improve relations and help organize the non-race events. While Daytona is open to all bikers, Harley-Davidson recognized the special importance of the rally to Harley riders.

The company became a major event sponsor. Harley rented the ballroom of the Hilton Hotel to display our model lineup and accessories. We also set up demonstration rides, which was a first in the industry at that time (more on Harley's involvement at Daytona in chapter 1). Soon, the Japanese companies set up their tents and offered rides, too. But only Harley showed up at the rally with employees, some of them factory engineers and service technicians, to talk bikes—customizing them, fixing them, riding them—with the revelers.

Judge Willie

Willie G. Davidson, Harley's head designer, and his staff like to serve as judges at the Daytona Ride-In Show. They often pick up ideas for future product design and new accessory products.

Harley separated itself from Japanese competitors in other ways, too. Daytona, known first and foremost for its racetrack, hosted motorcycle races during the rally week. All the Japanese bike companies were there (Kawasaki, Honda, Suzuki, and Yamaha) and a few European bike companies, too (Ducati, Triumph, and BMW). Harley did not participate. While the competition was racing around the Daytona track, we turned left on Orange Avenue and headed for the ocean. Daytona Beach became the focus of our activities—the food, the bikes, the music—and our race was held near the beach, where the action was.

Imagine the people that we had on the beach and the people they had at the speedway—very different crowds. The people who came to the beach were the serious bikers, our core customers.

The problems of the 1980s—rowdy bikers brawling with each other, townsfolk, and college kids on spring break—were resolved when Harley met with the Daytona chamber and police officials. We suggested ways to make it fun for the crowd, suggested that the accessory manufacturers pay license fees to hawk their wares, and let Daytona make money at the same time. Since that time, Harley has enjoyed a symbiotic relationship with Daytona and a warm reception each March.

The Daytona rally is extremely important to Harley-Davidson. It is the first major rally of the riding season. Like opening day at the ballpark, it is the beginning of the riding season. All the motorcycle parts manufacturers attend; it's a chance for them to show off their new products and accessories. It's a fun party, attracting hundreds of thousands of rabid bikers, and it is an ideal opportunity to bond with and support the Harley community.

The Rallies: Sturgis

The granddaddy of all rallies, Sturgis, too, first rose to prominence because of its motorcycle race.

In 1936, Clarence "Pappy" Hoel bought an Indian Motorcycle franchise in Sturgis, South Dakota, and formed the Jackpine Gypsies Motorcycle Club, which is still going strong today. (Pappy later became a Harley dealer.) On August 14, 1938, the Jackpine Gypsies held the first Sturgis motorcycle race on a dirt track with nine racers and a group of about 200 spectators.

The race became an annual tradition (except during World War II because of rationing) and attracted more and more riders each year. By the 1960s, the three-day rally had grown in popularity and was extended to a five-day event, later stretched to its current seven days in 1975. In 1979, the city began offering temporary vendors licenses—nine that first year—and that attracted more riders, who wanted to view all the cool accessories they could use to customize their bikes. Rally attendance began to grow dramatically.

Today, more than a half million people ride into the tiny town (population 6,442) on the edge of the Black Hills each August. For a single week, it is the center of the motorcycle universe, an annual pilgrimage for many.

Many others just come to watch half-mile dirt-track races, hill climbs, and drag races, and to shop. There are over 800 licensed vendors (who all pay a fee to the rally organizers). During this time, people listen to seven days' worth of nonstop music and drink more beer than the rest of the state of South Dakota does during the entire year. One of the local campgrounds sponsors a sunset ride sans clothing. The week gets a little crazy.

Why Sturgis? It is located in a central location of America that provides thousands of riders with hundreds of scenic roads to ride on the way to the event. It's a journey as well as a tradition.

Harley-Davidson uses the Sturgis rally to further bond with its customers. In addition to several tents, Harley-Davidson also sponsors the Ride-In Show, a series of contests where bikers enter their customized bikes in one of six categories.

Rebels With a Cause

Bikers tend to be a generous lot. Riders to Laconia, Daytona, and Sturgis each year generate thousands for the MDA, disabled veterans, and other charitable organizations. The annual Mayor's Ride in Sturgis, for instance, raises money for the local volunteer fire department. Actor Lorenzo Lamas organized the Rough Riders Rumble tour to benefit Walter Reed Army Medical Center.

It may seem quirky to see a burly biker dude giving a sidecar ride to a little kid, but on some level, many bikers are still out to prove to society that not all motorcycle riders are evil or crazy.

Large tents display the latest in MotorClothes and Motor Accessories, and Harley shows off its new bikes—all the new models are there (just a few weeks after they have been introduced to dealers at the annual dealer meeting). There are also demonstration rides throughout the week for those who want to try out the latest models.

Harley-Davidson supports Laconia, Daytona, Sturgis, and other rallies because it helps the company maintain the welfare of the Harley brand.

A Commitment to Your Customers

The tremendous effort Harley-Davidson puts in to participating in and supporting these rallies plays a part in the brand strategy to enhance Harley's strengths—heritage, tradition, and Americana. It also helps to maintain customer loyalty by giving the customer an experience, a lifestyle, something more than just a machine. Research shows that a majority of Harley owners will buy another Harley if they decide to purchase another motorcycle. But here is a scary thought: if just 5 percent of a company's customers choose to go to a competitor each year, even if the company's sales remain the same, that company's profits will fall by 25 percent or more (according to a complex formula that depends largely on the cost of new customer acquisition). The reason: it costs much more to sell a new customer than it does to sell a current customer. Bottom line, if a company wants to be more profitable, it must keep its current customers happy.

Now here's something comforting: companies that keep their current customers happy grow faster than other companies. Those happy customers tell their friends, who tell their friends, who tell their friends.

How to Bond With Customers

- Make the customer's experience with your company an event, like going to a big party.
- Make it easy for your customers to bring their friends along for the ride; that makes the party better for everyone.
- Create your own branded community where customers feel as if they are a part of the company.
- Make the customer service experience easy, straightforward, and pleasant.
- Encourage discussions about their experience with the product, and allow your customers to feel they contribute to the product development team.

But those customers can only be retained if they are loyal and motivated to resist competition. A satisfied customer—"Yeah, the product performed as I expected. Nothing special."—is not the same as a brand-loyal customer. With the next big competitor price reduction or snazzy ad campaign, that satisfied customer will walk.

Customer retention means creating satisfaction with the product's performance, yes. But it also means exceeding customer expectations, creating a special experience, a trust, a bond that transcends mere satisfaction and ascends to fulfillment, loyalty, and advocacy. At Harley, the sale truly begins *after* the sale.

Harley's commitment to its customers is sacrosanct. The Harley Owners Group's primary purpose is to provide the riders with a positive experience and build a bond between Harley and the riders. Dealers and HOG chapters sponsor rides just about every weekend of the year, weather permitting. Harley executives ride along and participate in events (not something executives of the competition do). They enjoy riding and talking with customers. To customers, these motorcycle events give a face to the name. Harley-Davidson becomes more than just a bike, a factory, or a business. It takes on a persona, an important element of the brand image. These rides humanize the brand.

Furthermore, this human involvement gives customers direct access to the Harley family: "The guy riding next to me is a technician at the Harley factory. Maybe I can talk to him about designing a better product." Riders spend time carefully examining the new designs. They offer suggestions and recommend new products. They make jokes, too. And why not? They are part of the Harley family.

Harley communicates with its family members frequently. Not in a pushy way, just to issue friendly reminders—the new models are in, there's a holiday sale on MotorClothes, that sort of thing—or an invitation to an event: "Come ride with us." Who doesn't like getting invited to a party?

It's this constant commitment to the customers that is most responsible for growing the Bar and Shield's loyal customer base.

Advocates for the Brand

The fundamental reason for brand welfare is to maintain customers' positive relationships with the brand over time. Design and manufacture a quality product and wrap it with outstanding customer service and reasons to use the product, and you gain a happy customer. Maintaining that relationship over time requires constant perseverance.

It is no coincidence that Harley aims three-fourths of its promotional dollars directly at its current customer base—not other bikers, not non-bikers, current customers. Harley strives to make the relationship with its customers so special, so gratifying, that those customers tell their friends. They become the best salespeople. They get so excited about the brand experience, their enjoyment of the brand associations and brand extensions, that they share those positive experiences with family and extended family, friends, colleagues, and strangers. They brag about how great it is to ride with other Harley owners. No, they never thought they could be a Harley rider, but then they heard from a friend how fun it is. Now they are crazy about riding, too, and they passionately recommend the experience to anyone who will listen.

Who needs advertising? Harley-Davidson has the best form of advertising there is: word of mouth.

The Japanese companies spend the majority of their promotion budgets interrupting people with TV ads, radio spots, and brochures, and they garner a small share of the biker market, especially those more interested in transport than fun. They attract novice bikers who believe it's better to start small before graduating to a big bike. And that is OK. There is a good chance they will get on a Harley someday, because their biker friends will tell them how much fun the Harley experience can be.

Harley-Davidson continuously arms its customers with the tools and information they need to become brand advocates. Then Harley lets them sell the brand. Some companies call it customer retention management (CRM). At Harley, it goes beyond retention. Harley-Davidson makes the experience of riding a motorcycle so rewarding that customers become devoted to the brand at every step of the relationship, from the anticipation that precedes the buying experience to the ongoing enjoyment of the product.

It works. The faithful are committed.

It is important that Harley customers feel good about the brand. To know that Harley is a good corporate citizen, to know that Harley sponsors the rallies where they have a good time, to know that Harley embraces the same ideals and the same values that they embrace further enriches the relationship. The bond grows stronger. Brand loyalty is maintained, enhanced, and rewarded.

The welfare of the brand is secure.

6
BRAND TEAM

Imagine: Your tie is off, your shirt unbuttoned before you're even inside your home. You stuff your legs through your jeans and into your boots and pull the leather jacket from the armchair. Three minutes, not more, and you are on the road with two hours of daylight remaining—plenty of time. The destination has yet to be decided. A twisty in the hills west of town? The beach road along the lake? Or an easy cruise down Main Street?

The destination is irrelevant, just a mark on a map. You ride for the alone time, for the freedom of it, the sheer rapture. It is the emptying of your emotional ashtray at the end of a long day behind a desk. Nine to five is their time. You sit in an office; you collect your data; you file your reports; you pay your dues. They own your time.

But not now; this is your time. You experience the precise alignment of the belly, the heart, and the mind—all wrapped around a silver Heritage Softail Classic with the chrome-laced spoke wheels and the wide whitewalls. The V-twin rumbles, its throaty voice in counterpoint to the hum from your wheels as they trace the curves.

Beside the road—a dot on the horizon at first but familiar as the distance narrows—is a bike. Its rider, arms akimbo, turns to you as you slow. The scene tells the story: the gas tank lid is up, and the rider has a sheepish look on his face.

Your destination is decided. You have a passenger now, and you turn your bike around. No matter that this is your alone time. No matter that your passenger rides a Japanese bike. You are part of a greater family, a team that includes all riders everywhere. Owning a motorcycle includes membership in the fraternity. Membership requires a responsibility to all other riders. It is the code.

By nature, we are tribal. Our tendency is to congregate, to cluster and come together for the greater good. No individual should always be expected to do it alone—ride, work, or live. We all depend upon others for their skills, their experience, their grit, to guide us on the path. In all things, we are part of a greater whole.

A team of people was responsible for the ideas, plans, and successes mentioned throughout this book. This chapter shows how we did it and provides some important advice to take away.

What Is a Brand Team?

The building of a brand takes all the members of the team—operations, finance, and marketing, from top management to the laborer on the assembly line, the vendors, and especially the dealers. All have to be working toward the same goal. It is a team effort.

Piles of books and hundreds of experts, from Vince Lombardi to Neil Armstrong to Peter Drucker, tout the value of teamwork. According to Vince, "Individual commitment to a group effort—that is what makes a team work, a company work, a society work, a civilization work." No argument there.

The principle behind teamwork is that the whole is greater than the sum of the individual parts. If two heads are better than one, then three must be better still. Team members build off the ideas and suggestions of others to create better ideas and suggestions. A brand team follows the same principles and stages of development as any other type of team.

The process of building a successful team begins with people—people who have similar interests and complementary skills, people who have the ability to sacrifice their personal goals for the common good. They must be collaborative. They must be accountable. And they must be enthusiastic for planning, implementing, and evaluating their efforts and correcting any mistakes.

An academic named Tuckman postulated that there are four stages of team development:[9]

1. Forming

2. Storming

3. Norming

4. Performing

All teams begin by forming. Serious issues aren't tackled at this stage; team members just gather information about each other, the task at hand, and how to approach it. Not a lot gets done yet.

During the storming stage, things get interesting. Different ideas compete for consideration—and so do personalities. A strong leader emerges, either by design (through corporate rank or appointment), by default (if the strongest personality prevails), or by election (if participants vote for one). The ideal leader is participatory, seeks consensus in decisions, and does not allow members to feel they are being judged.

At the norming stage, all members have had their say. All agree on common goals and a single plan. Some may have had to abandon their ideas and their opinions for the good of the team. But they all accept their responsibilities, and they all embrace common goals.

> "People who work together will win, whether against complex football defenses or the problems of modern society."
>
> —Vince Lombardi

Performing teams work as a single unit without real conflict or need for supervision. They are capable and motivated. Dissent is expected and encouraged but only as it is constructive and focused on team goals. Performing teams periodically revert to other stages as they react to changing circumstances. A new leader, for instance, may cause the team to revert to storming as team dynamics change. Performing teams achieve their goals sooner than teams at any other stage, but all four phases are necessary and inevitable in order for a team to meet goals and deliver results.

Good teams are important to a productive and healthy work environment:

- Teams build trust when team members complete their specific tasks.
- Teams build camaraderie among group members.
- Teams improve company morale as goals are met or even exceeded.
- Teams increase overall productivity.
- Teams create opportunities for personal growth.

The Harley Brand Team

The turnaround of Harley-Davidson was all about the team: the thirteen original investors, the dealer network, the vendor community, and the employees and their unions. All collaborated successfully. (Actually, not all. Those who were not good team members had to be redirected or replaced.)

"It's part of you."

Harleys have a voice—that low-pitched growl—that makes a Japanese bike sound like a dentist's drill. A Harley speaks to the rider, tells him of its condition and the condition of the road.

To a motorcycle owner, his Harley is like a horse was to a cowboy. It becomes an extension of who he is, of his lifestyle, of his soul. As actor Mickey Rourke says, "It's a personal thing that can't be described. It's part of you."[10]

When Harley-Davidson became an independent company, it was bleeding red in buckets. But spirits were high, and the marketing campaign proudly became: "Motorcycles. By the people, for the people."

Engineering and manufacturing were busy improving quality and designing future products. Finance was busy raising money to keep the company afloat. It was marketing's turn to step up and build the brand.

Marketing's start of the turnaround occurred in March of 1982, nine months after the buyout. Carmichael Lynch Advertising of Minneapolis became our advertising agency. They had served as Harley's sales promotion agency for a few years, so we had experience working with them.

Carmichael-Lynch used a unique structure that was perfect for Harley-Davidson. The agency had a separate team they called the Gas and Oil Division—a copywriter, art director, account manager, and their support staff—who all had experience in products that used gas and oil. Motorcycles were a good fit.

Step one was to get everyone on the same page. The Harley brand team spent a week in Minneapolis with the Gas and Oil Division. Our purpose: rescue the brand. We quickly got past the "how do you dos" and began poring over several hundred pages of documents. There were reviews of the industry, the competition, the products, sales and market share statistics, and previous advertising and promotion campaigns. It was important that we all had the same knowledge base.

We spent several days on a SWOT (strengths, weaknesses, opportunities, threats) analysis, looking at both Harley and our competitors. First, we looked at Harley-Davidson. What we saw wasn't pretty.

Harley Strengths	Harley Weaknesses
Heritage	Quality
Tradition	Money
All-American	Dealer relations at low ebb
Styling	Marketing
Image	Brand image

Heritage we had. Three generations of the Davidson family had been involved with the company. Tradition was solid—Harley had been in business since 1903 and had been at Sturgis and Daytona since their beginnings. We were definitely all-American, the last remaining motorcycle maker in the United States. Harley styling was classic, even iconic—evolutionary, not revolutionary. Our customers were loyal, people who would ride nothing but a Harley no matter what.

Image was the paradox. Every time a group of Harley riders got together, most people feared they were out for their monthly rape/burn/pillage quota. And to be honest, that rough and rowdy image was appealing to some riders. Yet many more were machine operators and construction workers, tradesmen and skilled laborers, and some were doctors and lawyers, bankers and accountants, engineers and entertainers. A diverse group constituted the Harley family, but the image was not one you could call "family friendly."

"Harley-Davidson. If I have to explain, you wouldn't understand."
—Harley T-shirt

Other weaknesses abounded. Though quality was improving, most people still thought that if it said Harley-Davidson on the gas tank, it must leak oil and need repair every 500 miles. The company had cash problems that frightened our lenders to the point that they were trying to get out of the deal at any cost. Our dealers were tired of fixing every Harley that came off the assembly line. Marketing struggled to change the Harley image but had no money to do it. And our bikes cost a lot more than comparable Japanese models.

Those were the strengths and weaknesses the brand team had to work with. Next, we examined our competition, and what we saw was disheartening, almost frightening.

Harley-Davidson	Competitors
Dealers are enthusiasts	Dealers are businessmen
Terrible quality	High quality
Premium price	Affordable price
Big bikes only	Full line of bikes
North American focus	International focus
No cash	Lots of cash

The Japanese were kicking our butts, no question about it. A quick glance at the market share figures confirmed that. According to R.L. Polk and Company, in 1980, Harley's market share of heavyweight motorcycles was 30.8 percent, meaning the competitors held 69.2 percent.

Worse still was the flooding of the market. Despite the downturn in the market after the buyout, the Japanese were still making thousands and thousands of bikes, small ones and heavyweights, and shipping them to the United States. The country was in the pits of a major recession, and rather than lay off their own workers, the Japanese manufacturers kept making lots and lots of bikes and exporting their excess product to the US market.

Senator Robert Kasten put it best when he claimed that the Japanese were simply "exporting unemployment":

> What has occurred here is a truly massive buildup of Japanese inventory that bears no relationship to US market needs . . . Japanese motorcycle manufacturers, rather than laying off their own workers, are maintaining high levels of production and are exporting the bulk of that production to the United States. In other words, the Japanese are exporting unemployment and that is not free trade.[11]

Whatever they were doing, it was killing Harley-Davidson. Fortunately, the ITC, at the urging of President Ronald Reagan, granted Harley a reprieve by imposing stiff tariffs on imported heavyweight bikes. It helped level the playing field temporarily. Most importantly, the ITC ruling granted Harley time to get its act together.

The brand team set out to describe the company's position in the market, something that could be used as a brand statement. It may seem like an easy thing to do, simply describe who you are in forty words or less, but it isn't. The brand statement had to be encompassing. It had to embody all that Harley stood for. It had to galvanize all who heard it.

We started by answering these three questions:

1. Who are we?

2. Who are our customers?

3. What do they want and expect from us?

Team members threw out ideas. Some described their personal attachment to their bikes. Others focused on the company.

"We sell the Harley lifestyle and experience."

"We serve selected market segments with a classic line of motorcycles."

"We make a growing line of motorcycles and branded products and services."

"We share the passion for freedom held by riders and encourage them to express their individuality through extraordinary motorcycle experiences."

The brand team spent five days in Minneapolis knocking around ideas, writing down slogans, crossing out this, and rewriting that. We finally came up with:

> Harley-Davidson manufactures big beautiful American motorcycles for motor enthusiasts who want their products to be symbols of strength, freedom, individuality, Americana, and who want to share and participate in the Harley-Davidson heritage, tradition, and mystique.

That was our base. It was a beginning.

Forming to Performing

In retrospect, the brand team followed Tuckman's format to a tee.

The forming began at our four-day meeting in Minneapolis with the ad agency's Gas and Oil Division. It had to be quick. We didn't allow much time for members of the team to get to know one another, just to exchange some contact information, and then we moved on. It did serve as an opportunity to see how each member of the team worked with others and how they responded to pressure.

We spent a lot of time storming. There were a lot of conflicting ideas and suggestions that didn't make sense. But this was not the time to discourage ideas, no matter how impractical. So we brainstormed and traded ideas and evaluated little, at least at the beginning stages.

I feel strongly that it is best to weed out people who are not likely to buy into new ideas—people who say things like, "We tried that, but it didn't work," or "That's a dumb idea, and it'll cost way too much"—and to do it quickly. Take them aside and tell them, "Here is what you need to do to fit in." Then give them a definite time frame—thirty days or six months—whatever it takes to get them turned around. If they don't fit in within that time, get rid of them.

> "Ideas should appear crazy before you explain them, not after."
>
> —Harley proverb

But I also believe that everybody has the right to be wrong. It's important to allow for failure, to take risks. Without risk, there is no reward. So I encouraged team members to explore new ideas, so long as the ideas contributed to the long-range goal.

After four intense days of storming, it did not take long to get into full swing in the norming stage. The brand team identified goals and set strategies quickly. All of us were committed to the company. Our enthusiasm bordered on elation—we were on our own, no more AMF and its ad agency telling us what we could and couldn't do. We developed a plan on which we all agreed, and we simply needed to go for it.

And that's when the brand team started really performing. The brand statement was only the beginning. The brand team was ultimately responsible for creating and developing the Harley Owners Group, securing licensing agreements, identifying and authorizing Motor Accessories and MotorClothes suppliers, and building the iconic Bar and Shield brand.

Brainstorming

The brand team/marketing group held a lot of brainstorming sessions with other teams to help build the brand. Whether about public relations, sales, sales promotion, advertising, service, or product design, brainstorming was critical to the creation of ideas and implementing strategies that built the brand.

There are good ways and bad ways to run a brainstorming session. Start with the group. Be sure they are all committed to the same goal—the same *single* goal. Don't try to solve the financial problem in the same session you're trying to solve the promotion problem. It's best to have a group of six to twelve people. More than that and some people don't get a chance to share their opinions. Fewer than that and you're missing opportunities.

Avoid being judgmental, or you discourage involvement. The more ideas, the better. Quantity is more important than quality, at least in the beginning. Yes, eventually those ideas need to be refined until they're practical, but naysayers need to be discouraged or eliminated.

Meet in the morning if you can. The mind is fresher in the morning. After lunch, people are more lethargic. Never present results to your boss after three in the afternoon. He's not fresh and is usually too busy putting out fires. The boss is less likely to take a risk late in the day.

Use a note taker, a nonparticipant who serves as scribe. Somebody should write down the agreements and ideas as they flow, making them easier to recall later. Sometimes, combining different ideas can lead to new ideas. Having a list to refer to helps in that process.

Be a facilitator more than a leader. Getting the best ideas out of all of the participants takes synergistic skills. Listening is more important than speaking. Understanding is more important than being understood. And have fun; team building can be a wonderful experience.

After the meeting, distribute the results to all departments. Keep everyone informed of what's going on. Others may add fodder that enhances those ideas hatched in your brainstorming session.

The Takeaways

Now that you know the wonderful story of how Harley-Davidson rebuilt its brand, here is some advice to take away:

- **Hire passion**—I am a firm believer in hiring passion. People who are passionate about their jobs don't work; to them, work is play. They become your most dedicated employees, and they give you the biggest return on your investment. They give you what I call "return on involvement."

- **Ride**—I strongly encouraged our employees to ride—into work, after work, on dealer-sponsored rides, to rallies around the country—anywhere and everywhere. Employees who are avid riders are most likely to be passionate about the company and passionate about their work. Hire people who use the product.

- **Don't hire puppets**—Hire people who are different from you, whose skill sets supplement your own, people who are comfortable working out of their element, wearing a variety of hats.

  At Harley, we had a policy of job swapping; workers would trade jobs with each other for an extended period of time. Accountants were asked to be part of product management; engineers joined the marketing department; manufacturing staff worked in purchasing and materials management. This practice not only developed future leaders but helped develop employees' empathy for each other's positions and responsibilities. Plus, it frequently produced outstanding ideas. As a bonus, it also allowed Harley to cover important positions while doing time-consuming hiring searches.

- **Use SWOT**—SWOT analysis is one of the best exercises you can use to develop ideas. Studying the strengths, weaknesses, opportunities, and threats of your company and your competition helps determine what your turf is. Ideas flow from there.

- **Identify barriers and eliminate them**—Again, SWOT analysis can help. Once a problem is known and understood, it can be resolved. Harley needed to triple its engineering staff and do it quickly, so we screened dozens of applicants for qualifications and then hired passion. Harley needed vendors to buy into the long-term growth plans that called for doubling sales in three years, and when one-fifth would not or could not go along, we found replacements.

- **Pick the place**—Fight on your own turf, not the competition's. The Japanese companies owned TV airtime at a time when Harley had little money. We didn't try to buy airtime since we couldn't; instead, we set out to own the rallies and major motorcycle events. This strategy also helped Harley bond with its customers. The Japanese companies touted their superior quality and revolutionary design. We didn't contest the points the Japanese companies were making; instead, we proclaimed our evolutionary classic styling and American heritage.

- **Turn negatives into positives**—Harley owners were perceived as rowdy, uncouth roughnecks; we built off that reputation to create one of rugged individualism. Harleys derisively were called hogs—slow, fat, and dirty; Harley named its owners group HOG. The competition made radical styling changes each year; Harley made subtle changes to launch new models that retained the classic Harley look.

- **Partner**—Be a partner with everyone who has an interest in what you do—suppliers, vendors, dealers, unions, shareholders, charities, community, everybody. If it's good for you, make it good for them. Create win-win scenarios whenever possible.

- **Be honest**—Face your weaknesses head-on. Be honest with your customers. Our quality was bad. OK, we acknowledged it. Then we fixed it. When it was better, we reassured our dealer network and thanked them for their patience during the years of poor quality. Only then did we make sure our customers were made aware of the improvements, too, with an advertising campaign that focused on our customers and reinforced their buying decision.

- **Be authentic**—Authenticity counts. It's not enough to shed the disco shirt for jeans and a black T-shirt. You have to ride. Attend rallies. Live the life. Harley-Davidson didn't just get close to its customers; we bonded with them. The customers became advocates of the brand. Happy customers are your best salespeople.

The Journey

The Harley-Davidson brand has endured the bad-boy image bestowed by Hollywood, suffered through years of poor quality, weathered the best the Japanese could throw at it, and staggered back from the brink of bankruptcy. Yet it remains a revered icon.

By recognizing the importance of the brand experience, extending the brand to a wider customer base, associating the brand with popular products, maintaining consistency at all brand touch points, paying back the community that built the brand, and relying on a team effort to conceptualize and cultivate the brand vision, the Bar and Shield has grown to symbolize all that is right and good about motorcycles: the product, the passion, the ride.

It was a long and difficult journey. Harley's employees, dealers, vendors, and management deserve the credit. I was privileged to play an integral part in the building of the brand for twenty-five years. Just one cog in the machine—a big, shiny, black and orange machine. And I am eternally grateful.

—Clyde the Glide
   Castle Rock, Colorado
   June 2012

NOTES

1. J. Josko Brakus, Bernd H. Schmitt, and Lia Zarantonello, "Brand Experience: What Is It? How Is It Measured? Does It Affect Loyalty?" *Journal of Marketing* 73, no. 3 (2009): 52.

2. Peter C. Reid, *Well Made in America: Lessons From Harley-Davidson on Being the Best* (New York: McGraw-Hill, 1990).

3. Peter C. Reid, "How Harley Beat Back the Japanese," *FORTUNE* (September 25, 1989). http://money.cnn.com/mag-azines/fortune/fortune_archive/1989/09/25/72503/index.htm.

4. Reid, *Well Made in America.*

5. Robert Grede, *5 Kick-Ass Strategies Every Business Needs* (Naperville, IL: Sourcebooks, 2006).

6. Philip Kotler and Kevin Lane Keller, *Marketing Management,* 12th ed. (Upper Saddle River, NJ: Prentice Hall, 2006).

7. Sam Moses, "He's Loose as a Goose and Flies on a Bike," *Sports Illustrated* (November 8, 1976).

8. A. H. Maslow, *Motivation and Personality* (New York: Harper, 1943).

9. Bruce W. Tuckman, "Developmental Sequence in Small Groups," *Psychological Bulletin*, 63, no. 6 (1965): 384–99.

10. BigPond, "Harley-Davidson The 'Marvel from Milwaukee,'" accessed April 3, 2012, http://203.36.31.67/Research/ Motorbikes/Harley-Davidson-The-Marvel-from-Milwauke e?PageletCategoryName=Research%2FMotorbikes%2FHar ley-Davidson-The-Marvel-from-Milwaukee.

11. Reid, *Well Made in America*, 87.

BIBLIOGRAPHY

Bolfert, Thomas C. *The Big Book of Harley-Davidson: Official Publication*. Milwaukee, WI: Harley-Davidson, 1989.

Davidson, Willie G. *100 Years of Harley-Davidson*. Boston: Bulfinch Press, 2002.

Grede, Robert. *5 Kick-Ass Strategies Every Business Needs*. Naperville, IL: Sourcebooks, 2006.

Kotler, Philip, and Kevin Lane Keller. *Marketing Management, 12th Edition*. Upper Saddle River, NJ: Prentice Hall, 2006.

Moses, Sam. "He's Loose as a Goose and Flies on a Bike." *Sports Illustrated* (November 8, 1976).

100 Years of Harley-Davidson Advertising. Boston: Bulfinch Press, 2002.

Reid, Peter C. *Well Made in America: Lessons from Harley-Davidson on Being the Best*. New York: McGraw-Hill, 1990.

INDEX

ABOUT THE AUTHOR

CLYDE FESSLER, retired vice president of business development for Harley-Davidson Motor Company, played an integral part in their dramatic turnaround.

Fessler joined Harley-Davidson in 1977 as the advertising and promotions manager and soon was promoted to director of marketing services. In that position, he led the establishment of Harley Owners Group (HOG), which now has over a million members and is the largest enthusiast club in the world.

As general sales manager in the early 1980s, he established new policies and programs, many of which are still in effect today. As director of licensing, Clyde created a new business that has received national recognition, enhancing the brand to the general public as well as adding substantial financial value to Harley-Davidson.

As vice president of general merchandise, he repositioned the rider accessory department and led the MotorClothes team from $20 million in annual sales to over $100 million in a period of five years. As vice president of Motor Accessories, he developed the plan and strategy that doubled the business in three years and tripled it in five years.

In his role as vice president of business development, Clyde played a key part in developing strategic direction for the company, sponsoring programs like Motorcycle Rentals and the Rider's Edge safety training program.

Clyde is a graduate of the University of Notre Dame. He served on the board of trustees for the American Motorcyclist Association and the Motorcycle Safety Foundation. He also served as an active liaison between the Muscular Dystrophy Association and Harley-Davidson, a relationship that has generated over $80 million in donations since 1981.

Clyde retired from Harley-Davidson in early 2002 and is now active as a marketing consultant and motivational speaker. He enjoys fulfilling his dreams by exploring the world on one of his four Harley-Davidson motorcycles with his wife, Joan.

Books from Allworth Press

Allworth Press is an imprint of Skyhorse Publishing, Inc. Selected titles are listed below.

The Art of Digital Branding, Revised Edition
by Ian Cocoran (6 x 9, 272 pages, paperback, $19.95)

Brand Thinking and Other Noble Pursuits
by Debbie Millman (6 x 9, 320 pages, paperback, $19.95)

Career Solutions for Creative People
by Dr. Ronda Ormont (6 x 9, 320 pages, paperback, $27.50)

Corporate Creativity: Developing an Innovative Organization
by Thomas Lockwood and Thomas Walton (6 x 9, 256 pages, paperback, $24.95)

Effective Leadership for Nonprofit Organizations
by Thomas Wolf (6 x 9, 192 pages, paperback, $16.95)

Emotional Branding, Revised Edition
by Marc Gobe (6 x 9, 344 pages, paperback, $19.95)

From Idea to Exit: The Entrepreneurial Journey
by Jeffrey Weber (6 x 9, 272 pages, paperback, $19.95)

Infectious: How to Connect Deeply and Unleash the Energetic Leader Within
by Achim Nowak (6 x 9, 256 pages, paperback, $19.95)

Intentional Leadership: 12 Lenses for Focusing Strengths, Managing Weaknesses, and Achieving Your Purpose
by Jane A. G. Kise (7 x 10, 200 pages, paperback, $19.95)

Millennial Rules: How to Sell, Serve, Surprise & Stand Out in a Digital World
by T. Scott Gross (6 x 9, 208 pages, paperback, $16.95)

Peak Business Performance Under Pressure
by Bill Driscoll (6 x 9, 224 pages, paperback, $19.95)

The Pocket Small Business Owner's Guide to Building Your Business
by Kevin Devine (5 ¼ x 8 ¼, 256 pages, paperback, $14.95)

The Pocket Small Business Owner's Guide to Business Plans
by Brian Hill and Dee Power (5 ½ x 8 ¼, 224 pages, paperback, $14.95)

The Pocket Small Business Owner's Guide to Negotiating
by Kevin Devine (5 ½ x 8 ¼, 224 pages, paperback, $14.95)

To see our complete catalog or to order online, please visit *www.allworth.com*.